A Christian Counselor's Primer On...

For helping those who struggle with......

A series of Resource Manuals for Counselors, Pastors, Teachers, Altar Workers, & all those who serve to comfort and equip the Body of Christ.

Addictions & CoDependency

Book Four

Written by
Debbye Graafsma, bcpc

Awakened!!
Awakened to Grow
Counsel. Classes. Retreats
awakenedtogrow.com

DISCLAIMER

The lesson materials contained in this primer notebook are provided for informational purposes only. These materials, and any or all accompanying materials published by the author, are not in any way intended to diagnose, treat, or evaluate mental illness; nor are they a substitute for professional counseling and care. Those who suffer from the difficulties covered in "A Christian Counselor's Primer On ..." series of booklets should seek additional counsel for their unique situation. Optimally, the materials should be worked through with a trained professional counselor.

The information contained herein is provided for educational purposes only. The user assumes all risks. Debbye Graafsma, Awakened to Grow, and their affiliates deny responsibility for any and all misuses of the information provided.

Awakened to Grow Ministries
P.O. Box 546
Indian Trail, NC 28079
Website: awakenedtogrow.com

A Christian Counselor's Primer on Addictions & Codependency; A series of resources for those who help others... Book 4 (ISBN - 978-0-9893214-0-2)

©2014 Debbye Graafsma, Awakened to Grow. No portion of this manuscript, nor its accompanying materials may be reproduced or stored by any means or in any format without the written expressed consent of the owners.

A Christian Counselor's Primer on...Addictions & Codependency
Table of Contents

Introduction -- 7

Section One.
    Basic Principles of Growth and Healing-- 9

Section Two.
    Let's Talk About Addictions-- 19
    Let's Talk About Codependency -- 27

Section Three.
    Dealing with Addictions & Codependency-- 37

Section Four.
    Assessment and Discovery Tools-- 81

Section Five.
    The Counselor's Role in the Healing Journey--------------------------------------- 103

    Required Choices to Heal --- 119

Section Six.
    What the Bible teaches about Addictions & Codependency-------------------- 135

Section Seven.
    Scriptural Prayer and Supportive Materials-- 145

Introduction

Dear Fellow Servant,

If you are reading this, you are either considering purchasing this little hand-book or, have already purchased it... Perhaps you are deliberating how you will incorporate it into your ministry or counseling practice. It is my hope that the information contained here will become a tool, to enable and equip you to more effectively hear and Holy Spirit when it comes to helping others. Not only that; but it is my goal to make your efforts even more fruitful, by providing you with Biblical background and lessons to accompany counseling materials.

Each book in this series: "A Christian Counselor's Primer on...." contains current information relevant to its subject, suggested methods of treatment, as well as a series of charts on its topic that I have developed over the past twenty years in private pastoral counseling practice. Over this period of time, I have found my clients respond more positively when I chart out the truths regarding spiritual and emotional conditions. Doing this allows a person to identify their own experience as it relates to the picture presented to them. We then discuss and learn in conversational one-on-one discipling.

Additionally, I have also developed self-assessments and questionnaires for my clients, in order to aid and speed individual discovery. I have included those assessments and/or questionnaires in these hand-books as they relate to the subjects at hand.

At the end of each hand-book are suggested reading lists for you, the counselor, allowing further study, as well as for the client, allowing personal growth and development.

In Christian circles, it is sometimes too easy to give "pat" answers, or "quick fixes," without seeing actual healing and growth take place in the lives of those we are seeking to serve. Such situations render the client feeling inept, or worse, without enough "faith" to find solution. The fact that you are looking at this booklet exempts you from the circles in which those damaging office visits occur. Thank you for your desire to serve: helping and bringing healing to those who are wounded.

That being said, please allow me take a couple of moments to encourage you.

The ministry of providing a safe place for counsel is a vital one. So much brokenness exists in our society today; so much pain. And yet, only one person out of every four people who are referred to a counseling office will actually make the call and follow-through to keep the appointment. And, of those in that 25 percentile, only around half will actually commit to applying the training they receive in sessions, realizing change and growth. That means that together, as counselors, all of us have about a 13% chance of helping anyone! Believe it or not, that is really good news! After all, just one transformed life can change the world!!

Imagine. What could happen if thirteen out of every one hundred people in your sphere of influence became impassioned and empowered to grow, not only emotionally, but spiritually as well?

Years ago, General Motors' famed inventor and head of research, Charles Kettering, made a very wise declaration in describing how his department approached the concept of designing need-meeting vehicles. He said, "A problem well-defined is half-solved." Not only is this statement true when it comes to designing cars, but it is also true when it comes to the process of learning to choose well in living.

When a client can see the "why" of their struggle in growth and healing, they are more than half-way to discovering the repentant heart and desire to change they need to acquire more healing and therefore, health in their Christian Walk! An encounter with God is then just steps away! Hopefully, using the materials contained here will make than encounter a reality!

In the beginning of each volume, I explain a little about how the Father God's principles of healing work when it comes to emotional healing and spiritual development; with each volume building on the prior volume's teaching. Hopefully, this will help you to discover a sense of empowerment and personal mission. After all, that's why each of us began in this helping ministry……

It is my hope to help you and bless you!

Blessings!

Debbye Graafsma, M.Div., D.Min., bcpc
Awakened to Grow Ministries

Section One
Basic Principles of Growth and Healing
(for Books 1-4; Jesus' parable, "The Sower and the Soil")

There are twelve handbooks in the "A Christian Counselor's Primer on...." series. Each of these "quick-study" texts is designed to provide an overview of the subject presented. In discussing the ministry of helping others, it is important that we handle each subject from a Scriptural viewpoint. For books 1-4, we will consider the first parable Jesus Christ told during His ministry on earth: "The Sower and the Soil" as a springboard for basic understanding.

There is such hope and encouragement to be drawn from this parable. And the fact that it was the first parable Jesus told, also gives us a glimpse of the attitude of Abba Father towards us – even when we are in the worst of conditions.

The idea of healing the hearts of men and women began with Jesus. Continually, throughout His ministry on earth, our God spoke to the very roots and cause of the Pain and dysfunction each of us carry: our baggage, if you will. It is His method to say, "You have heard it said – but *I say to you*...." And then He finishes the statement with something that changes the entire perspective on whatever subject He was speaking.

Jesus came to heal. Jesus came to restore. Jesus came to redeem and rebuild those things lost and broken; those parts of us deemed as beyond repair.

The parable of the Sower is particularly precious in my own life, because the Holy Spirit used it in my own life to challenge my personal depth meter when it comes to emotional and spiritual development.

And let me just say this as we begin: Spiritual development and Emotional maturity cannot be separated. It is impossible to become a healthy, emotionally congruent individual, without finding ourselves at a crossroads of sorts. What will I do with the spiritual issues that stir in my soul when I decide I want to experience "more?" What answers will I allow to pervade and influence my mind and heart? By the same token, personal spiritual development cannot become a reality, unless I choose to yield yet again to the Holy Spirit of the Living God, and allow Him to challenge, confront, and change the attitudes and patterns of my dysfunctional past; allow Him to mold and form on deeper and deeper core levels, His nature and Personality within me....

Jesus Christ was a master Storyteller. In imparting Life-truths, He would weave a story that people related to and were fascinated by. The Sower and the Soil is one of my favorites.

Jesus explained this particular parable as being about the human heart; or what we would describe the soul. *(The human soul, is comprised of our mind, will and emotions; what we think, choose and feel.)*

Before we go to the parable, let me share a couple of charts with you, that I hope will serve you well in your desire to help others. When I first began counseling, these were some of the first I developed, and I find I use each of them at least once a day, even now.

The first chart, is the description of the Levels of Relationship and Communication. This is a basic chart that defines the difference between IQ, Intelligence Quotient, and EQ, Emotional Quotient. Emotional Quotient, or Emotional Intelligence, as it is being referred to these days, has to do with one's ability to relate to other people. EQ has to do with the deeper levels of living we all experience with the people we are closest to in relationships.

Jesus referred to the Emotional Quotient, as the "Heart of Man."

Please consider the IQ/EQ chart below.

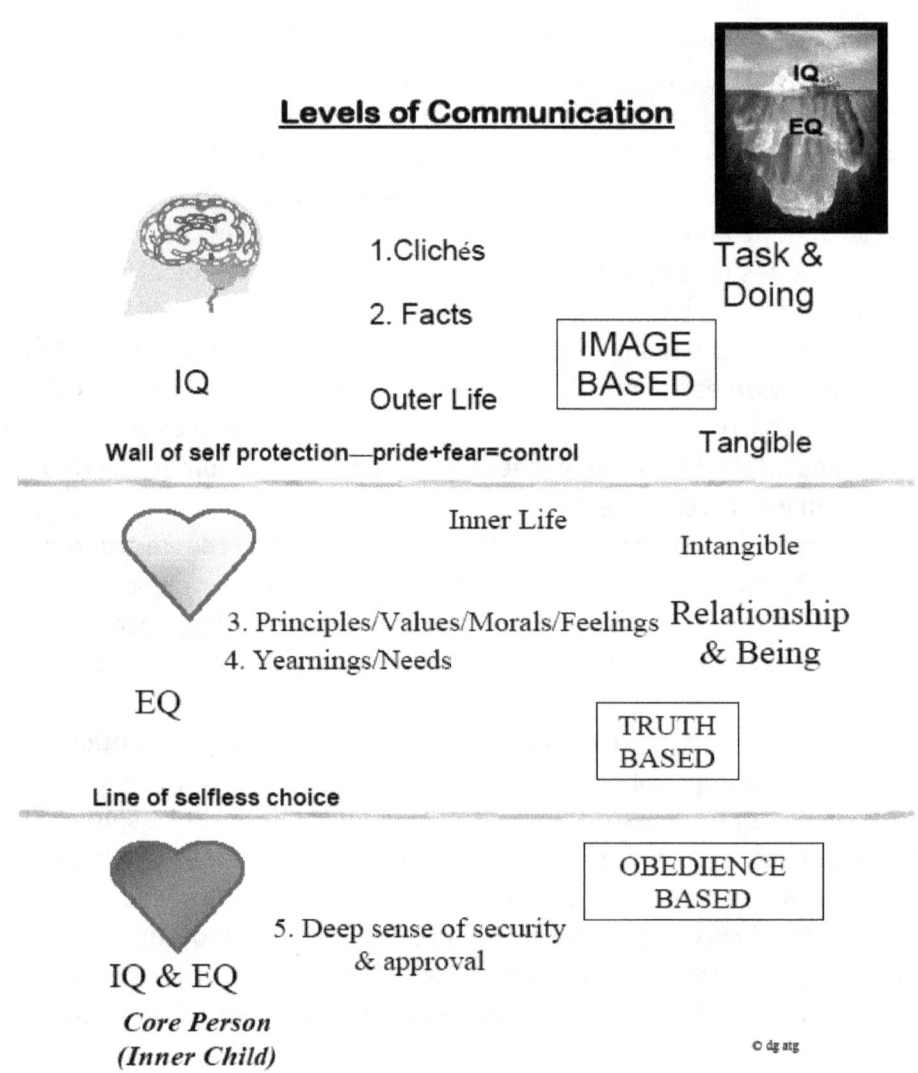

When we study this chart, we discover the differing depths of relationship each of us experience in our lives.

Level 1 = Cliches		These are the people we meet once on an elevator, or in a crowded room, and make **surface-level conversation** with, experiencing no fear or sense of risk.
Level 2= Facts		These are the relationships we encounter in our lives who require **a little more expenditure from us – but still without emotional impartation.** For example, when we are in school, we must memorize and repeat the facts. How well we remember many of the facts determines our Intelligence Quotient. (That is, "are we intelligent, able to apply the facts?" Also, "how well do our life achievements 'stack up' against others' lives, etc.")

A life lived on only levels 1 and 2 will be image based, success oriented, shallow in nature, and dependent upon performance orientation.

Between levels 2 and 3, there exists a Wall of Self-Protection. The wall is comprised of Pride and/or Fear. Simply put, Fear + Pride = Control. Most of us construct our personal wall in pre-puberty, or just after, depending upon the comparisons we make between our "nest" and the "nests" of those in our friendship circle, and how our own sense of "normal" compares to the "normal" of our friends and acquaintances.

Level 3 =	A *man* will experience Level 3 of relationships when he is able to determine his personal **principles and values**, and express them to his companions. A *woman* will experience Level 3 in relationships when she is able to express her **morals and feelings** to her companions. There are reasons for these differences in approaching this level of relationship differently; gender being the main reason.
Level 4 =	**Yearnings and needs** are what make up the deepest part of our being. In this level, we are able to share our hopes and dreams as they relate to our future. These are the deepest perceived needs we carry; many times without expression.

A life lived incorporating levels 3 and 4 into daily experience, will manifest the Personhood of a well-bonded individual. Such a person has chosen to cease trying to "hold to the image" of who he or she believes must be portrayed in day to day living.

However, what actually fuels, or gives power to, the Emotional Quotient levels of our lives is the substance of Truth. In places where we have learned to believe our experiences as being the source of Truth, we will develop broken trust and an inability to relate to others in a healthy way. (This is something we all do.)

When we become believers in Christ, the Holy Spirit begins the process of personal transformation; bringing comfort, healing, change and growth. In the midst of this maturation, there comes a point in the life of every believer when he or she is confronted with the realization of the disparities and contrasts between what our experiences and taught us to be true, and the Truth of God's Word.

If a person chooses to cling to the perceptions he or she has always believed; the person's own conclusions of "truth;" then the processes of emotional development and spiritual maturation cease. Sadly, when this type of refusal to the Spirit's formation occurs, any future discoveries the believer receives will be tainted by that refusal; influenced by elements of fear and legalism.

In contrast, when a believer is willing to take the risk of trusting God for their emotional development, the Holy Spirit (the Helper and Teacher) continues the process of healthy emotional and spiritual development by breathing courage into the soul. He then will confront the believer with the need to exchange those inward perceptions of "truth" for Abba Father's Truth. When our "truth," or perception, is traded for God the Father's Truth, the Bible becomes a template learning how to live the life of a believer. At that point of growth, the Word of God becomes real to us; more than mental assent.

At that point, *His Truth* becomes voluntarily traded for *our truth*. *His Truth* is durable, unshakable, and trustworthy.

Then, as we continue our lives in Jesus Christ, at some future point of our development, we each must come to another place of choosing. This second choice presents us with as question. Will we allow the Holy Spirit to deepen our resolve and obedience with God?

This is the choice to move forward without looking back. It is at this point we discover that we are disciples of Jesus Christ. This second choice, or "wall," if you will, is the fear which confronts us when we seek to give our lives away, or invest our efforts into a cause that will benefit others. When the choice towards discipleship is make, we become willing to offer something of ourselves to God, and to others, simply for the common good. We do it with a sense of purpose and fulfillment, and it is an offering that comes from deep within.

This deepest part of us, I refer to as the Core, or Inner Child.

Now, let's take a look at how those levels of communication affect our personal relationships.

The journey of the Christian life is one that takes us inward, as well as one that focuses our intentions outward. The inward journey of personal Discovery and Empowerment requires the confronting of imprinting, pain and experiences with cause us to be malformed in our emotional growth and development. This is what only the Creator can re-imprint and heal. After all, God is the only Perfect Parent. The outward journey determines the direction of our personal development. It also maintains our balance. In this journey, the Holy Spirit teaches us how to express His care and love for others – without pretense or fear, as disciples of the Living God.

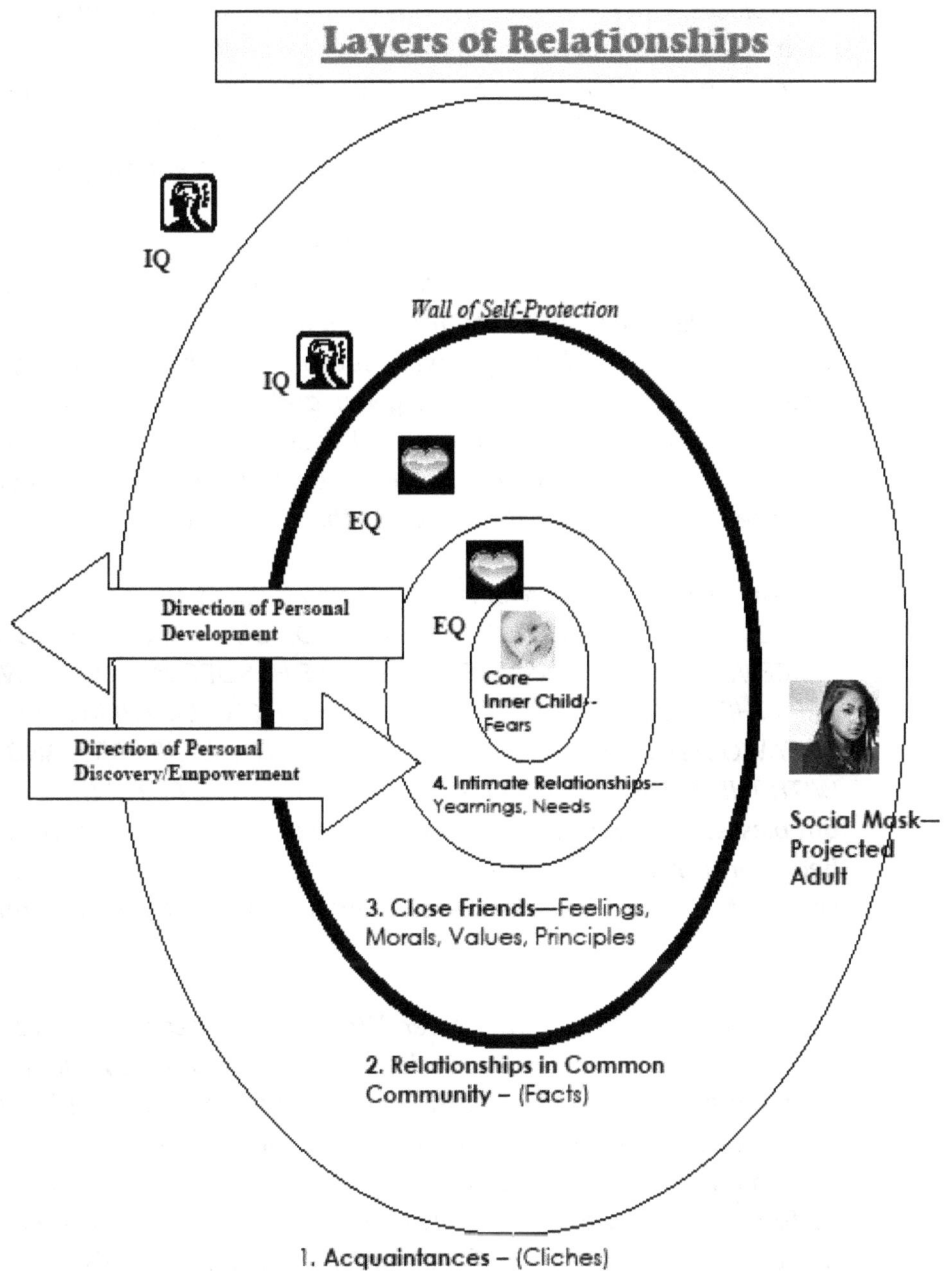

Jesus continually referred to this growth and discovery process. In Matthew 13, our Savior told a parable about a sower, his seed, and the soil.

"That day Jesus went out of the house and was sitting by the sea. And large crowds gathered to Him, so He got into a boat and sat down, and the whole crowd was standing on the beach. And He spoke many things to them in parables, saying, "Behold, the sower went out to sow; and as he sowed, some seeds fell beside the road, and the birds came and ate them up. Others fell on the

rocky places, where they did not have much soil; and immediately they sprang up, because they had no depth of soil. But when the sun had risen, they were scorched; and because they had no root, they withered away. Others fell among the thorns, and the thorns came up and choked them out. And others fell on the good soil and yielded a crop, some a hundredfold, some sixty, and some thirty. He who has ears, let him hear.

And the disciples came and said to Him, "Why do You speak to them in parables?" Jesus answered them, "To you it has been granted to know the mysteries of the kingdom of heaven, but to them it has not been granted. For whoever has, to him more shall be given, and he will have an abundance; but whoever does not have, even what he has shall be taken away from him. Therefore I speak to them in parables; because while seeing they do not see, and while hearing they do not hear, nor do they understand.

In their case the prophecy of Isaiah is being fulfilled, which says, YOU WILL KEEP ON HEARING, BUT WILL NOT UNDERSTAND; YOU WILL ON SEEING, BUT WILL NOT PERCEIVE; FOR THE HEART OF THIS PEOPLE HAS BECOME DULL, WITH THEIR EARS THEY SCARCELY HEAR, AND THEY HAVE CLOSED THEIR EYES, OTHERWISE THEY WOULD SEE WITH THEIR EYES, HEAR WITH THEIR EARS, AND UNDERSTAND WITH THEIR HEART AND RETURN, AND I WOULD HEAL THEM.'
But blessed are your eyes, because they see; and your ears, because they hear. For truly I say to you that many prophets and righteous men desired to see what you see, and did not see it, and to hear what you hear, and did not hear it.

Hear then the parable of the sower. When anyone hears the word of the kingdom and does not understand it, the evil one comes and snatches away what has been sown in his heart. This is the one on whom seed was sown beside the road. The one on whom seed was sown on the rocky places, this is the man who hears the word and immediately receives it with joy; yet he has no firm root in himself, but is only temporary, and when affliction or persecution arises because of the word, immediately he falls away. And the one on whom seed was sown among the thorns, this is the man who hears the word, and the worry of the world and the deceitfulness of wealth choke the word, and it becomes unfruitful. And the one on whom seed was sown on the good soil, this is the man who hears the word and understands it; who indeed bears fruit and brings forth, some a hundredfold, some sixty, and some thirty."

In this parable, Jesus speaks of four different levels of soil. He likens each level of soil to a condition of a person's soul. As you read, consider and remember the four levels of communication, and the four levels of relationship.

1. Trampled, hardened – describing the soul of a person who does not understand Kingdom life, and who dismisses the Word as not being necessary for living.

2. Rocky, shallow – describing the soul of a person who has many hard and stony places in their heart. They can hear the Truth and have a desire to learn, until they are corrected or confronted. They lack the ability to follow through, and things outside the Presence of God gain attention and loyalty.

3. Weedy, thorny – describing the soul of a person who has battles with distraction in their desire to walk a solid walk with Jesus.

4. Good soil – 30, 60 and 100 fold – describing the soul of a person who receives the seed of God's Truth with an open heart and responds with obedience and teach-ability. Notice that good soil has degrees of fruitfulness.

In this parable, Jesus refers to these differing qualities of soil as being descriptive of the state of the heart of man. This was the first parable Jesus told in His ministry on earth; which makes it highly significant in looking at how God views the condition of our soul when it comes to our ability to relate to Him and to Truth. For me personally, it reminds me that Abba Father made man and woman in His image, placing them in the Garden of Eden to cultivate it and keep it. That would mean that our God has always been a cultivator; a Gardener of the soul, if you will.

What is most encouraging about this parable is that soil quality can be changed. Just like a physical garden, hard work is involved to break up the hard soil, remove the stones, and weeds. And, just like a physical garden, fertilizer is added to soften and enrich the soil. In relational terms, the "fertilizer" which enriches the soil of the heart of man, would be the life lessons (God-given) we take away from the painful experiences in our lives.

As we walk through the first five books in the primer series, please remember the levels of soil, and how they relate to the levels of communication and relationships. Over the past twenty years, I have used these comparisons in the ministry of pastoral counseling; seeing results in the lives of believers as well as disciples.

The four types of soil Jesus referred to in the Sower's parable, directly relate to the four levels of communication and relationship, listed and shown below.

IQ	**1. Cliches** **2. Facts**	*Image based – intelligence* *Task and Doing oriented*
EQ	**3. Values, Principles (male)** **Morals, Feelings (female)** **4. Yearnings and Needs**	*Truth based – heart of man* *Relationship and Be-ing oriented*
Core	**Inner Child**	*Real self/spiritual perceptions* *Obedience and Inner Approval oriented*

There are many areas of relational living which correspond to these four levels of relationship. For a more detailed addressing of this subject, and to pinpoint a person's placement in growth, please consider utilizing the G.E.M.S. Personal Assessment Tool, (Section M), by Debbye Graafsma. *(Available through Awakened to Grow, or online.)*

When a person lives in a healthy state, individual Personhood is expressed through the whole being. This is called Congruency. On a practical level, the person portrays the same personality in all settings of living. They are strong enough in their Core to withstand the pressures and intimidations of varying environments.

When we come to Christ, becoming believers for the first time, very rarely is anyone congruent. That process begins when we choose to yield to the Spirit of God, allowing Him access and permission to shape us into the likeness of Christ.

In considering these truths, I have provided a chart on the next page, which combines the work of cultivation or gardening, with the condition of the soil on each level. It is my hope it will encourage you as you encounter believers as well as disciples in your ministry as a helper/counselor.

The Sower and the Seed: Becoming A Cultivated & Well Watered Garden

"The Lord will guide you continually, and satisfy your soul in drought, and strengthen your bones, and you shall be like a watered garden, and like a spring of water, whose waters do not fail." Isaiah 58:11

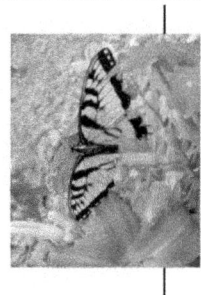

The Parable: Matthew 13:3-9 and 18-23

Type of Soil Vs 3-9	Jesus' Meaning vs 18-23	Condition of the Heart	A Gardener's Solution	Spiritual Application
1. Seed on the wayside -- was devoured by birds	Not understood. Devil steals it. Survivor mentality	Numb, Trodden down. By reason of conditioning has become rock hard feels used.	Soak with water. Break up crusty earth. Dig deep earth. Dig. Remove rocks. Add fertilizer and conditioners before planting. Feed well.	Has learned to believe a lie. Life experiences have wounded and closed the heart. (emotionally and spiritually)
2. Seed on stony places -- no depth, withered by elements	Receives, but has no depth in himself to make application, is offended by difficulty and falls away only. No joy. "Tell me what the rules are – I'll do that."	Unaware of deeper possibilities. Too many hard things with no understanding or ability to resolve. Functioning plants well.	Water well to loosen earth. Remove stones. Dig down to rock. Add fertilizer and conditioners. Feed	Sees the stones. Feel stuck. Difficulties argue with the love of God. The heart wants to trust, but fears repetition of pain. (trusts self most)
3. Seed among thorns -- new growth crowded by weeds	Receives, but has so many other things "going on right now" any application is squeezed out, becomes unfruitful	Aware of deeper growth. Drawn by Holy Spirit – is easily distracted by obligations and responsibilities. Content to maintain on surface but lives unfulfilled	Weed out crowded growth beds. Spade around plants for aerating soil. Add fertilizer. Condition soil. Water well. Monitor for sprouts of weed seeds not pulled on first try.	Is weed aware, assumes they are normal – is used to emotional clutter. Fearful of Change – task oriented for security. (works based. Condemnation focused, fear driven)
4. Seed on good ground -- yielded a crop	Receives, understands, allows it to grow, and bears life-fruit	Open and vulnerable. Teachable, receiving truth and making application personal changes daily indicate growth	Maintain weed free status. Maintain condition of soil. Regular cultivation and aeration for health. New plantings and pruning as applicable.	Maturity takes time, growth takes time. There are no substitutes. Discipleship involves discovery. Emotional health and spiritual maturity cannot be separated. Daily maintenance will ensure continued development.

Section Two
Let's Talk About Addiction

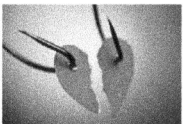

"What is an Addiction? How Do I Recognize one?"

The word "addiction" is widely used in our culture. In the 1970's the term came to the public forefront, with the rise of illegal drug usage. Since that time, the term has come to encompass a great many more substances and levels of living.

The Mirriam Webster Dictionary defines "addiction" as:

1. The quality or state of being addicted.
2. A compulsive need for and use of a habit-forming substance (as heroin, nicotine, or alcohol) characterized by tolerance and by well-defined physiological symptoms upon withdrawal
3. A persistent compulsive use of a substance known by the user to be harmful
4. A strong and harmful need to regularly have something (such as a drug) or do something (such as gamble)
5. An unusually great interest in something or a need to do or have something

For our purposes, we can define an addiction then in its simplest form, as an out-of-control appetite, or developed obsession. With this definition, the term includes a great many behaviors and substances. In counseling forums, the suffix "aholic" has come to be added to behavioral descriptions. A few examples of this present practice would be: "shopaholic, workaholic, alcoholic, text-aholic, phone-aholic, sex-aholic, learn-aholic, clean-aholic, smoke-aholic, sleep-aholic, food-aholic, tv/media-aholics, golf-aholic, video game-aholic and many more. Even though the terms might make you smile, they are far from humorous, especially for those who live with such a person in their home.

Addictions, and the tendency toward addiction, can be passed down in family generations, simply changing form as the years go by. For example if a man's father was an alcoholic, he might choose not to drink alcohol, but then succumb to a gambling addiction. The same propensity towards Addiction is present in his life, with personal issues still remaining unaddressed. Or, a woman's mother was a drug addict, or sexual addict, and she traded the shame-based overt addiction for a more acceptable one, like workaholism.

An Addiction is diagnosed by a clinician when a person continues at any point in life to continue to seek and/or engage in a practice or in using a chemical, despite negative consequences (such as a loss of job, debt, or physical problems).

Addictions first manifest in a person's life in the form of a craving. The craving in itself is not dangerous. Continued satisfaction of the craving, however, will strengthen and reinforce that craving over time. This is the beginning of an obsession, which then becomes a dependency, or addiction.

In my own experience as a pastoral counselor, I have noticed that certain personality types will find it easier to develop an addiction, while others tend towards Codependency. For my own purposes, a person with a tendency toward addiction is a reference to a life-approach attitude. There are many influencers which compound this tendency, and can cause this kind of attitude to become apparent. With most addictions and addictive personalities, the younger the behavior begins, the more likely it will continue, simply because the person lacks inner resources to tell themselves "no." Risk factors:

1. a family history of addiction
2. a perceived trauma
3. depression
4. anxiety

Many times, an addiction is an attempt to self-medicate an anxiety disorder of depression, or to prevent the person from feeling emotional or physical pain.

Signals of addiction:
1. A person sets a limit for a certain behavior, and then repeatedly exceeds or ignores or explains away that limit
2. A person realizes they are thinking about a repeated activity with high frequency
3. Changes in social or intimate relationships, so that a person changes their associations, or withdraws and is less interested in people or activities that formerly brought pleasure to them.

Eventually, in an addict's life, the addiction takes control, with the addict's appetites and emotions demanding to become the center of personal orbit for every person who comes into the addict's circle. This is especially true when it comes to family situations. When this happens, there no longer are individuals within the family structure, working and serving together as family. Instead, the Addiction has become the center of the family's orbit, and high levels of dysfunction set in, creating unhealthy relationships.

Wherever Addiction exists in relationship, there also exists Codependency. One cannot exist without the other.

Forms of Addiction

Alcohol	Drugs, prescription or illegal	Smoking
Eating disorders	Gambling	Shopping/Spending
Sexual addictions	Caffeine	Clothes
Obsessions and Compulsions	Adrenaline	Chemicals
Sniffing fumes	Approval	Control
Power	Media	Body Building
Sugar/Carbs	Exercise	Pornography
Self (Hobbies/Interests)	Plastic Surgery	Travel

Addiction gains its foothold in a person's life because of personal choices and "see-thoughts." One of the most common seed-thoughts is the idea and/or viewpoint that the addict feels they are an exception to the rules of living. Many times, an addict will develop the attitude they are "different," above the rest," or "outside the circle" when it comes to social groups. Sometimes a person will tell themselves that if a "really big break will happen" then their life will become what they wish it would be – until then, they will engage in this activity, and just stay in a waiting pattern. This tendency to hold on the dangerous "seed-thoughts" eventually leads to the disregarding of all need for responsibility in the life.

> **A recent study found that employees with substance abuse, when compared with non-addicted colleagues were found more often to be late, be absent, use sick benefits, file for worker's compensation, and be involved in accidents.**

Facts About Addiction

1. Addiction is a specific biological disorder of the reward systems in the brain, that has permanently altered the survival system, and the motivational priority system of an individual.

2. Addiction has a component of Denial, in which the person with the addiction is blind to the pain and burden which their addiction is placing on the lives of those around them.

3. One of the main hallmarks of an addiction is the continual and progressive use of an activity or substance, even in the face of adverse consequences. These consequences are debated, rationalized, or minimalized.

4. The beginning place of all addictions is emotional dis-regulation – meaning the person has difficulty regulating their feelings, and they seek solutions to their emotional state – and then the "brain switch" is thrown "on" towards Addiction.

5. Nothing seems to get the attention of an addict except the loss, or the threat of losing something or someone they consider valuable in their life. Sometimes, this kind of tough love, many times called an "intervention," is the only method of helping an addict discover their need for change.

6. Studies show that tendency towards addictions is usually generational, and although some are trying to prove that there is an "addiction gene," such proof is as of yet unobtainable. There is, however, evidence showing addictions can "run in a family." – although the forms of addiction can change from one generation to another.

7. Most addicted individuals translate the provision or enforcement of boundaries in their personal relationships as a communication of Rejection or a withdrawing of care. Most addictive personalities only respond to expressions of love requiring no response or reciprocation, perceiving this to be normal.

8. Addictions form in secret places, and are usually lied about, even though all the symptoms are visible, and readily apparent. The addict sees their addiction as an escape – many times with a filter of fantasy or surrealism and/or denial. This causes a numbness to ensue – even when conflict or confrontation happen.

Specific Substances and Medical Illnesses Associated with Their Usage/Dependence

Cannabis (Marijuana)   respiratory disorders, decreased pulmonary function, increased risk of emphysema and pulmonary cardiac arrest, cardiac abnormalities, premature ventricular contractions, decreased sperm count and motility, menstrual abnormalities, loss of cognitive brain function

Stimulants   sudden death, cardiac arrhythmias, fibrillation, infarction, hypertensive crisis, pulmonary edema, nasal septum perforation, chronic rhinitis, pulmonary infections, HIV, hepatitis (with intravenous usage)

Opiates   tuberculosis, generalized malnutrition, blood-borne virus transmission, staph infections, bacterial infections, abscess, pulmonary fibrosis

Reasons People Become Addicts

1. Un-health in family relationships
2. Unable to sustain emotional responsibilities – lack of tooling
3. Personality weaknesses
    Fear of losing control
    Inflexible thinking
    Perfectionism
    Low self-worth
    Helplessness)
4. Cultural pressures to perform, or conform to an image; criticism
5. Stress and trauma (rape, abuse, molestation, injustices)
6. Anxiety, Depression, or Insomnia
7. Family History
8. Chronic Pain or fear of pain
9. Loneliness
10. A community of addicts that accepts them

Applauded Addictions

Money Matters
~ Preoccupation with investing, hoarding and amassing a fortune
~ Gambling
~ Risk-taking
~ Collecting,/acquiring valuables
~ Keeping up with the Joneses
~ Binge shopping
~ Controlling others through money

Work/Play
nent on the job
~ Busyholism
~ Pursuit of academic degrees
~ Preoccupation with self-improvement
~ Over zealous homemaking, cooking, cleaning
~ Daydreaming, fantasizing
~ Music, TV, videos, computers
~ Sports

Wellness and Health
~ Body Building
~ Exercise
~ Diet and weight management
~ Medical treatment, tests, surgeries
~ Personal Hygiene
~ Hypochondria
~ Megavitamins
~ Sun Tanning

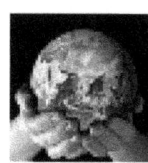
Service & Voluntarism
~ Martyr syndrome
~ Cause groups
~ Charity, church work
~ Loaning money to other people
~ Rescue relationships
~ Rescue professions

Relationships
~ Hero worship
~ Worry about others
~ Sexual activity
~ Super mom and dad
~ Friendships
~ People-pleasing addiction
~ Marital fighting

Perfectionism
~ Cosmetic surgery
~ Appearance, clothes
~ Order, organization
~ Toxiphobia (a fear of contaminants)
~ Unrealistic standards of performance
~ List making
~ House cleaning
~ Preoccupation with structures, rules, and rituals

Let's Talk About Codependency

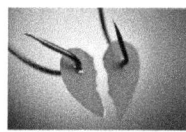

"What is Codependency? How Do I Recognize it?"

"Codependency" is a descriptive term, developed in the 1960's to describe the collective condition of spouses of alcoholics. The first term used was actually "co-alcoholics," but once research was expanded to the general public, it was discovered that the characteristics also described an enormous percentage of the population. In fact, as research has continued into the present, it has been discovered that anyone who grows up with an addict in their background, is probably codependent!

Over the years, the concept of Codependency has expanded into a definition which describes a dysfunctional pattern of living and problem solving developed during childhood by family mandates and pressures, the most common of which is "Don't show; don't tell."

In fact, codependent behavior is learned by observing it, copying it, and receiving approval for it in a dysfunctional family. Then, as the patterns become ingrained, they are repeated; passed on to the next generation. In fact, in many churches, Codependency is praised as being what God expects of those who believe in Him.

In adult living, codependents experience a greater vulnerability to enter a relationship with people who are emotionally unavailable, needy, undependable, and/or dependent. In response, the person dealing with Codependency begins to try to prevent their unhappiness. The codependent deals with fears of losing the relationship, and begins to feel responsible for the person's anger, even absorbing criticism. The codependent loses touch with their original identity over time, without addressing their own needs and development. This is how the relationship between an addict and a codependent many times begins.

The bad news is: almost everyone deals with a small amount of Codependency. It becomes debilitating if left untreated, destroying identity, and developing hopelessness in a person's life. And the good news?

Codependency can be un-learned. Healthy, creative and healing life-patterns can be learned.

Living life without Codependency is the original manner in which Father God created us to live.

> *"You have no control over what the other guy does. You only have control over what you do."*
> — A. J. Kitt

Characteristics of Codependency

1. **Painful emotions.** The stress of having to have it all together constantly, even in the midst of personal emotional difficulty, causes stress, and complicates negative thoughts and feelings. Most codependents deal with a low sense of personal value, and oftentimes operate in anxiety; having to do things "just right," fearful of making mistakes, experiencing rejection/abandonment/being alone. When the emotional burden becomes too great, the person will become numb/unfeeling.

2. **"I have to do it all."** Codependents are good at being hyper-responsible, and feel they must prove their personal value. For this reason, they will overstep and over-commit, many times past the point of maintaining their own mental/emotional health, in order to meet a goal or satisfy a need in relationships. Many codependents then, as a result deal with a sense of failure, a sense of being trapped, anger and resentment, discouragement, disillusionment, hopelessness and futility.

3. **The inability to say "no."** Part of a codependent's silent code of ethics includes the expectation to maintain the happiness and fulfillment of all those within their circle of relationship. Codependents many times assume responsibility for the feelings of others. They accept responsibility and blame for situations and attitudes, when there is no need to do so. In order to maintain this behavior, many codependents become "martyrs," in attitude, and can be extremely difficult to know and understand. Codependent people have difficulty "dividing the blame" when something goes wrong; they tend to approach situations with an "all or nothing" mindset.

4. **Fixations.** When a person is codependent, they will spend a lot of time considering how to make others happy. Due to their own fears, they can fall into the trap of fixating on how they wish life would become, and many times, trying to make it become so. They do this to avoid dealing with their present realities. In truth, even though this behavior might work temporarily, it prevents the codependent from actually experiencing health and healing in relationships.

5. **Becoming the "Happiness Guru."** Due to family upbringing, and the imprinted behaviors in a codependent's childhood, most truly believe they are expected (and many times they *are*) to become the "glue" person in the family – filling in all the gaps, taking care of all the details, while maintaining a smiling and unruffled exterior. In Christian circles, this behavior has even become praised as the sign of godliness. Nothing could be further from the truth. Most codependents fulfill this particular role because they believe they don't have a choice except to do so. Most codependents find it difficult to reply "no," to requests for their involvement; they become afraid of losing relationships. The identity of most codependent persons is based on how well they have accommodated the needs of others.

6. **Protective Care-giving.** Codependents tend to make noble choices, and those choices are applauded by others. The only problem is, a codependent person will ignore their own physical and emotional limitations in order to meet the needs of others. A codependent will also identify with a needy person's difficulties to the point that personal objectivity in his/her own life. Codependents also will try to force another person to choose health, wanting to help that person out of their pain. These attitudes and actions are perceived as controlling behavior. Codependents absorb responsibilities for other's choices and, most of the time, feel overloaded.

7. **Problems with relationships.** It is almost impossible for a codependent person to trust others on a deep level, even though they possess a deep hunger for such relationships. Most codependents keep their relationships with others at a distance, not allowing themselves to know or be fully known. This type of closeness, or intimacy, feels threatening. Most codependents deal with large amounts of Shame in their relationships. As a result, toxic amounts of false guilt bully the codependent with fears of rejection, conflict, judgment, and disapproval.

8. **Inability to feel secure when alone.** Most codependents will deny their dislike of being alone. The truth is, however, that most have difficulty experiencing deep rest or fulfillment without having someone in their company. Usually, a codependent will feel unspoken expectations emanating from those around them; and resent those expectations. But then, when the person is alone, emotional emptiness presents itself. Most codependents have difficulty recognizing and allowing themselves to live as individuals, each with unique and distinct identity.

9. **Little or no personal value.** Codependents continually have the sense that they are "not good enough." They will compare themselves to the people around them, and always come up short. Many codependents try to mask this emotion with a false sense of superiority. The truth is, they feel insufficient, insignificant, unattractive or without value. Driving these emotions is a great deal of Shame. Additionally, the majority of codependents feel compelled towards perfectionism. In actuality, perfectionism is a reasonable defense mechanism. For example, a perfect environment serves as protection against feeling inferior, and reinforce personal value.

10. **Defensiveness.** When a person is codependent, it becomes necessary to defend and define one's opinion of other's actions and words. When disagreement occurs, a codependent person will have either whole-hearted agreement, or defensive reactions. Receiving others' approval is extremely important, and disagreement is perceived as rejection. For this reason, a codependent person is threatened by conflict, and feels the need to maintain peace.

11. **Issues with Control.** Everyone wants to feel confident in their surroundings. Additionally, we all need to have some sense of control regarding what is happening in our lives and relationships. Codependent people deal with a greater sense of needing to maintain control than others. The problem is that codependents never feel as though they have caught up on their responsibilities. Many will develop an addiction to deal with this sense of not measuring up. Additionally, it is difficult for a codependent person to share their feelings with others. A codependent person need to make sure they have the "pulse" on events happening around them, usually to the point of control, in order to feel safe and secure.

12. **Manipulation.** Because a codependent person needs to feel safe, and works hard in order to obtain and maintain a sense of approval from others, they will many times use guilt and obligation to motivate other people. The fact is, a codependent secretly needs others to treat them in a certain manner in order to provide their personal sense of security. This is the "repayment" side of the codependent's people-pleasing and care-taking behaviors. People do things the way the codependent wants them to. As a result, most codependents are perceived as bossy and controlling.

13. **Unhealthy communication.** A codependent person has difficulty expressing their needs, thoughts and feelings. Most are not in touch with their own emotions, so experience emotional unavailability. Still others, might be in touch with their emotions, but find it nearly impossible to voice them, because there are afraid what they say will cause conflict. In this regard, codependents would rather live dishonestly, pretending that everything is "just fine." In this way, Fear reinforces the person's sense of being trapped.

14. **Insecurity.** Codependent people expect others to help them to feel secure and confident regarding themselves. The fear of being alone, or of being perceived as incomplete, serves as an emotional driver. Most codependents become isolated and/or depressed when they spend too much time alone. When a codependent is in a relationship with an abusive person, it is difficult for them to end the relationship, because the personal need to avoid being alone is so predominate.

15. **Denial.** Because Codependency is a learned behavior, and the codependent's sense of approval and acceptance is fed by the praise and affirmation of others, most codependent people consider themselves to be carrying out normal expectations. They are, most of the time, in a place of refusing to see their situation as a problem. After all, they are really very capable. Who else could do what they do? Or, they must continue to do what they do, because someone in their circle "doesn't get it," or "won't step up." This approach to the issue is called denial. Most codependents will not reach out to others for help, and have difficulty allowing others to help when it is offered. Self-sufficiency serves to reinforce their denial, as well as prevent any vulnerability in relationships.

    The sad thing is, for a codependent, it is just a matter of time before they are no longer able to continue their behavior. One of these outcomes is guaranteed to happen:
    a. A physical condition will prevent them from continue "doing it all."
    b. They will experience an emotional breakdown.
    c. Patterns of behavior will cause the alienation and loss of present relationships from whom they have come to draw identity.

> *"Codependents are reactionaries.*
> *They overreact. They under-react.*
> *But rarely do they act.*
> *They react to the problems, pains,*
> *lives, and behaviors of others.*
> *They react to their own problems,*
> *pains, and behaviors."*
> — Melody Beattie

Addiction and Codependency Work Together
in the Family Setting

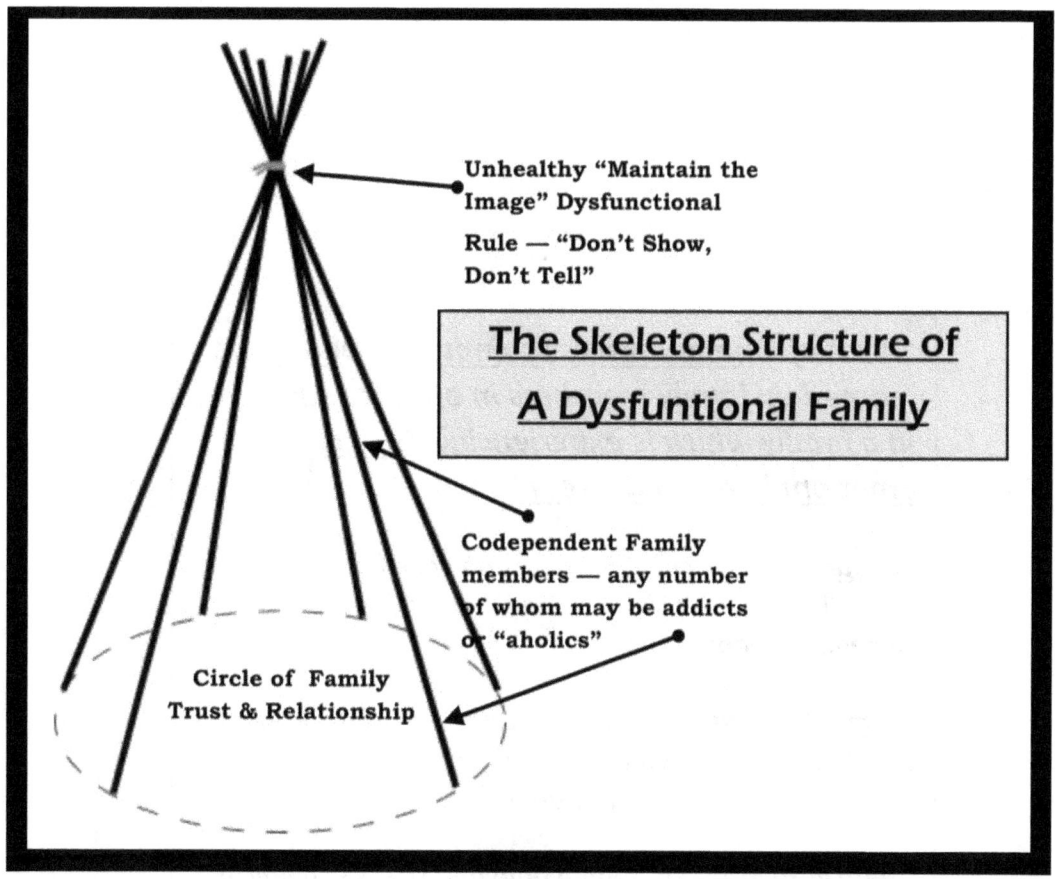

Addiction and Codependency always come in tandem to one another, many times with roles reversing back and forth between two people within the same family. All members of the family learn to facilitate the happiness and appetites of those addicted within the group. The members of the family are dependent upon each other emotionally for support. However, the dependency is not a healthy one. In a healthy setting, each pole (person) would be able to stand alone without help.

At the top of the tee pee, signifying mental agreement, the rule to "Maintain the Image" ties the family members together. There are two elements to this rule, which has worked in the development of every dysfunctional family in history. Those two elements are:

1. "Don't show" – meaning   It is unacceptable to allow people outside the family circle to know facts and information that might embarrass family, or diminish public opinion of family.

2. "Don't tell" -- meaning   It is unacceptable to express unhappiness or disapproval of anyone *inside* the family circle to anyone *outside* of the family circle. To do so means to risk rejection. This expression is seen as disloyalty and disrespect, especially if one is revealing the inner-workings of abusive behaviors or addiction.

Codependency –

"A set of *maladaptive, *compulsive behaviors learned by family members in order to survive in a family which is experiencing *great emotional pain and stress."

*maladaptive - *inability to develop behaviors prompting the ability to take care of oneself in areas of living. Unhealthy adaptation.*

*compulsive – a psychological state in which a person acts against their own will, better judgment and/or conscious desires, driven by an overriding fear or impulse.

*sources of great emotional pain and stress - chemical dependency; chronic mental illness; chronic physical illness; physical abuse; sexual abuse; emotional abuse; divorce; hypercritical and/or non-loving environment.

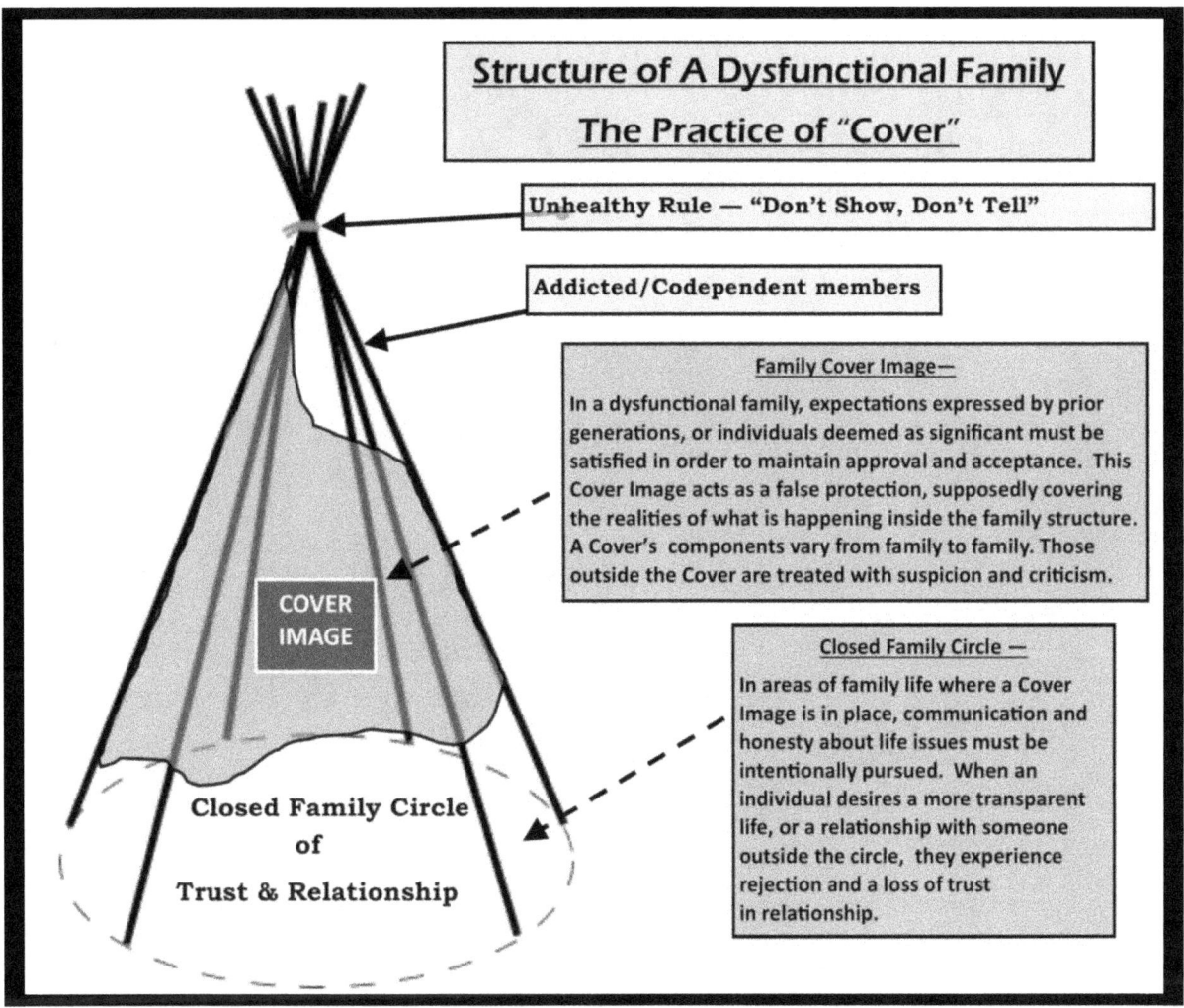

It takes a lot of effort to gain the trust of a dysfunctional family. It usually happens as a result of relationship failure, divorce, or death within the family. It is usually at those traumatic moments that member of such a household will be willing to admit help and counsel is needed.

When a member of the dysfunctional family seeks to become healthy, it is necessary to walk away from the unhealthy rules and dependent nature of the family unit. When that member does choose to change, refusal to accept the person's viewpoints and perceptions as being true will be the general family reaction. (To accept the family member's perception, and validate it as true, the requirement follows for change. Most dysfunctional families are too fragile to accept and pursue change as a whole. It usually occurs in one or two members only.)

In order to become healthy, the person choosing to make changes must come to terms with the attitudes and emotional expectations of the dysfunctional family unit, and be resolved to grow even in the face of Rejection and/or Distancing from family members.

Principle: Dysfunction never responds to Truth with acceptance, agreement, approval, or application.

Section Three
Dealing with Addiction & Codependency

Inside the Mind of an Addict

When we think about Addiction, it is important that we realize that persons who are addicted to substances and/or activities always have a unique way of looking at things.

All addicts are narcissists. The emotions and appetites which drive an addict, are also expected to drive and set the tone for all who come into the addict's circle of influence.

For every addict, common steps have occurred in getting the person to the place where they are now living. In order to fully help a client become un-stuck and able to move forward into health and wholeness, it is crucial to identify the timing of each of these steps. Additionally it is necessary to help the client decipher their emotions during the moments of those steps, as well as the personal choices he or she made regarding their own value and purpose during those moments.

Step One

The person is born. The setting into which they were placed; environment atmosphere; emotional and relational history of the family. How did the person see their personal

value? Did they grow up feeling important? Did their parents like them? What behavior was modelled for them? Did abuse occur? In regard to each of these questions, what did they feel about happened? What conclusions did they come to because of what they experienced?

Step Two

A traumatic event, or long-term traumatic relationship take place. In helping the client to decipher the events and how they felt about those events, you will be unravelling the

foundational reasons for their addiction. The stronghold for any addiction is found in these first experiences. The second place to find clues is within the person's fantasy. This mental ritual is a pattern a person uses to imagine life without the pain of their trauma. (They are unconsciously seeking emotional healing.)

Step Three

The person is halted in the process of walking through the Steps of Grief. Memories of the traumatic event hold the person's thought patterns in limbo. Or, the person begins to walk through the steps, and becomes mired down, cycling and stalled, unable to move forward to Resolution. The person recalls the quality of life they experienced before the trauma and/or loss occurred and feels emotionally un-tooled; powerless. Life becomes divided in the person's mind; between "before" and "after."

Step Three

True emotional development is halted, and the person constructs walls of False Identity. The person experiences an emotional hunger and is unable to find lasting relationship to completely fill the void within. To meet felt needs, the person will conduct a "search;" sometimes with relationships; sometimes with work; sometimes with substances. Patterns of behavior are developed, reinforcing hard lessons learned. All the while, the True Identity of the person is waiting behind the protective wall, waiting for approval and intentional development. Supposed development happening beyond the wall serves as a "survivor" self; a projected form of the person; stronger and more able to cope. This stage is maintained, many times for years, until the person experiences an intervention, another deep loss, or a breakdown due to exhaustion.

Note: *When a trauma occurs, the affected person immediately begins to journey through the Steps of Grief. When the process is halted/slowed, this immobility will manifest in the person's emotional development. Sometimes, survivors are very adept at masking the insecurity they feel inwardly. For those around them, one might even seem to "flip" between a stronger self, and a weaker, wounded self. In such cases, the stronger self is the mask, or projected adult, and the person's true identity is that of the weaker, more emotional self.*

Addiction are the means through which the traumatized person seeks to self-medicate their unprocessed grief. For actual healing to take place, a traumatized person must walk through personal discovery. It cannot be done alone, or in isolation. James 5:16 teaches us that emotional healing done God's way, must happen in safe community. The decision to embark on this type of journey must begin as a choice from the addicted person's heart. No one can force growth, or discovery. Additionally, true maturity cannot be rushed.

The Integration of All Parts

"And the very God of peace sanctify you wholly;
and I pray God your whole spirit and soul and body
be preserved blameless unto the coming of our Lord Jesus Christ."
I Thessalonians 5:23

In biblical times, it was generally understood there was a definite connection between the health of the physical body, and the condition of the soul. In our times, the medical sciences are finding this to be true as well. In fact, many physical conditions have feel found by the health community to be worsened when a person experiences stress. Such conditions include: obesity, heart disease, Alzheimer's disease, diabetes, depression, gastrointestinal problems, asthma, as well as some forms of cancer.

Man is a three-part being: Spirit, Soul, and Body. Each of these elements has its own qualities, and yet is integrated into man's entire existence. Each part affects the whole. When one part is healthy, it influences the other two parts with vitality. When one part is unhealthy, it influences the other two parts as well.

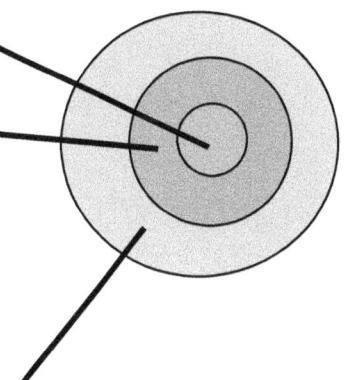

The Human Spirit – This part of man must be reborn into the spiritual realm, in order to experience life. The spirit of man consists of intuition, perception, and conscience. It is the part of man aware of the spiritual realm. Unseen and when born again, is eternal.

The Human Soul – This part of man is also unseen. It consists of the mind (thoughts), will (choices), and emotions (feelings). Personality and Beliefs reside here. It is the part of man more keenly aware of the physical realm than the spiritual realm. It is the area in which man wars to choose good/refuse evil. Those elements of the soul surrendered to the Holy Spirit's leadership (sanctified) are eternal. Seat of the appetites.

The Human Body -- This is the vessel; the tangible "earth-suit" which carries the real inner person. It is subject to the laws and deterioration of the physical realm, and must be maintained and stewarded. It is sight, hearing, touching, tasting, and smelling. This part of man is not eternal, and is the vehicle which satisfies his appetites.

Note: The battle and work for emotional health
and wholeness takes place within the soul (mind, will & emotions).

© dcg,atg

"One drink is too many, and
1,000 drinks are not enough."
Alcoholics Anonymous Slogan

How the Soul Becomes Disjointed

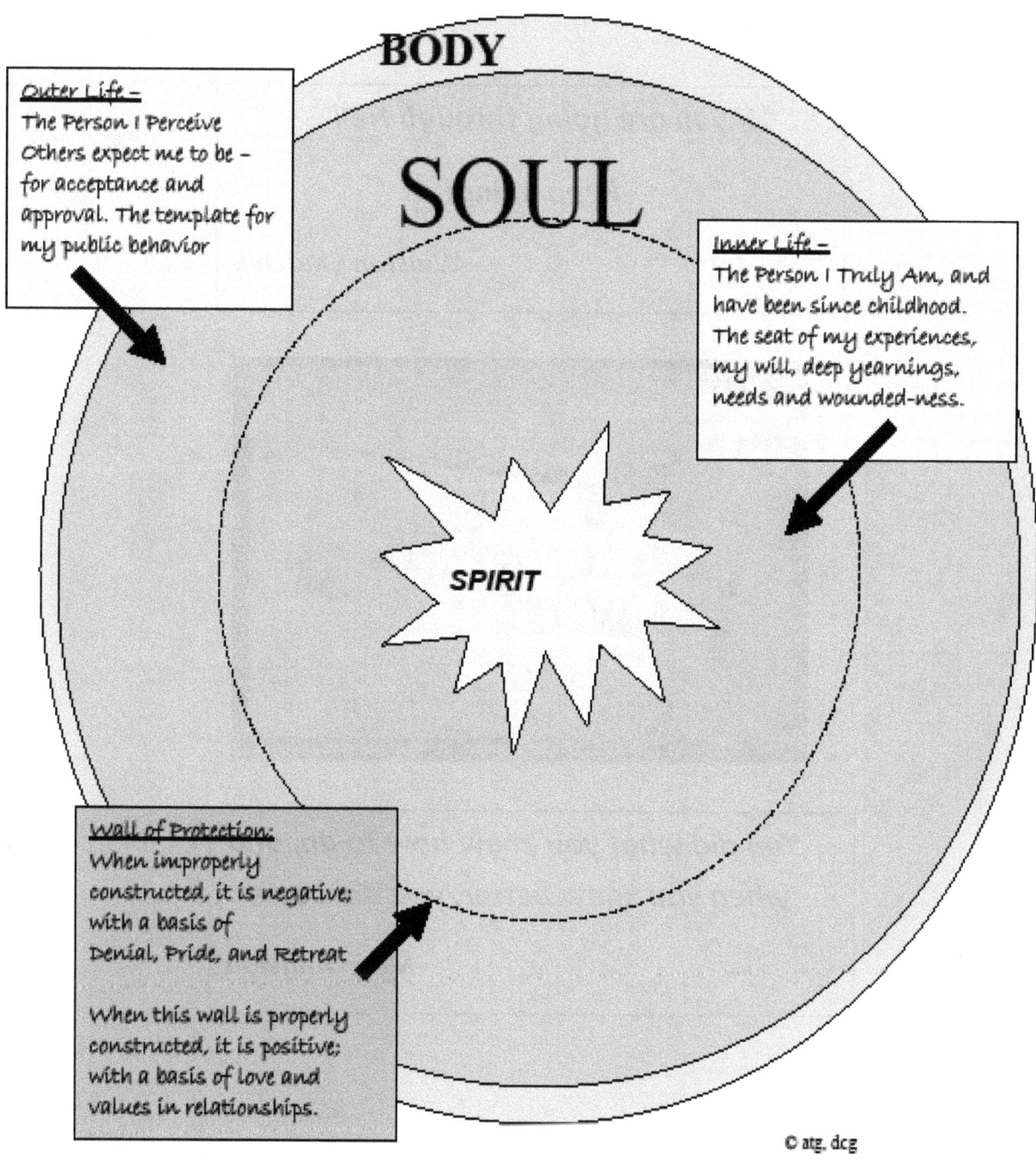

The outer part of the soul eventually becomes the "survivor," while the inner part of the soul holds the most vulnerable parts of the person. The Wall of Protection is based upon our own defensiveness; ability to protect ourselves; taking control.

> *If you are going through Hell –*
>
> *Keep going!*
>
> *--Winston Churchill*

> *You did what you knew how to do, and when you knew better, you did better.*
>
> *--Maya Angelou*

The Survivor vs. Real Self

Survivor Personality

Survivor Characteristics
- Emotional "power"
- Decision making
- Limited feeling & expression
- Demanding
- Must be heard
- Exerts control
- Conditional approval
- Guarded by: anger/withdrawal
- Stern/strict/can be abusive
- Rules/justice based
- Center of orbit/anger

In order for healthy living to occur, the false empowerment within the survivor personality must be dismantled. For this to happen properly, the Wall of Self-Protection must be exchanged for appropriate and healthy boundaries in relationships.

Wall of Self-Protection. Constructed of Fear and/or Pride (Fear + Pride = Control)

IQ / EQ

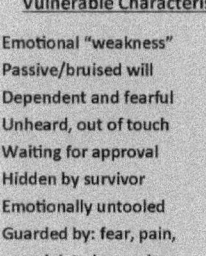

Automatic Self-Protective Defense Mechanisms

Elements of Denial manifest as a choice to adjust to the environment with an IQ or EQ personality style

Hidden/Vulnerable Personality

Vulnerable Characteristics
- Emotional "weakness"
- Passive/bruised will
- Dependent and fearful
- Unheard, out of touch
- Waiting for approval
- Hidden by survivor
- Emotionally untooled
- Guarded by: fear, pain, complaint, depression, bitterness, anger

In order for healthy living to occur, the hidden core personality of the inner child, must be validated and given voice to communicate emotions and perceptions. This most vulnerable personality must then be strengthened to stand to take its place in life management and decision-marking.

© dg/atg

Each of us can recognize within ourselves the quandary described in the chart above. The Survivor Personality is actually an Inner Bully in the experience of most of my clients. It is usually an unwilling copy of faulty adult modeling the person experienced during formative years. The person has learned to reject his or her Real Self, seeking to copy the faulty pattern. Many times, I will ask a client to study the chart and tell me where they might be out of touch with the Hidden/Vulnerable part of their personality. We then discuss the wall of Self-Protection, and how the devices of Denial/Defense Mechanisms actually play into their situation. It can take several sessions for a client to come to discovery. So don't be discouraged or get into a hurry, seeking to make healing happen too quickly. Allow the person to make discovery and encounter Truth.

On the following page, is a charted description of the gears of Self-Hatred. Self-Hatred is the catalyst which fuels the Survivor Self, and teaches the Real Self to allow itself to be shut away.

The Mechanisms of Self-Hatred

There is a great deal of struggle in the inner life of both the addict and the codependent. Neither person is living in day-to-day reality. Both have learned to exist/survive, doing whatever is needed to gain the approval of those in their relationship circle. When the codependent fails to keep everyone happy, it is compounded many times by issues of Self-Hatred. The longer the life-pattern persists, the longer the process to unravel it; the more involved in re-programming thought patterns, and experiencing freedom. A compounded possibility also exists. The addict and the codependent may each develop emotional unavailability.

The Development of Emotional Unavailability

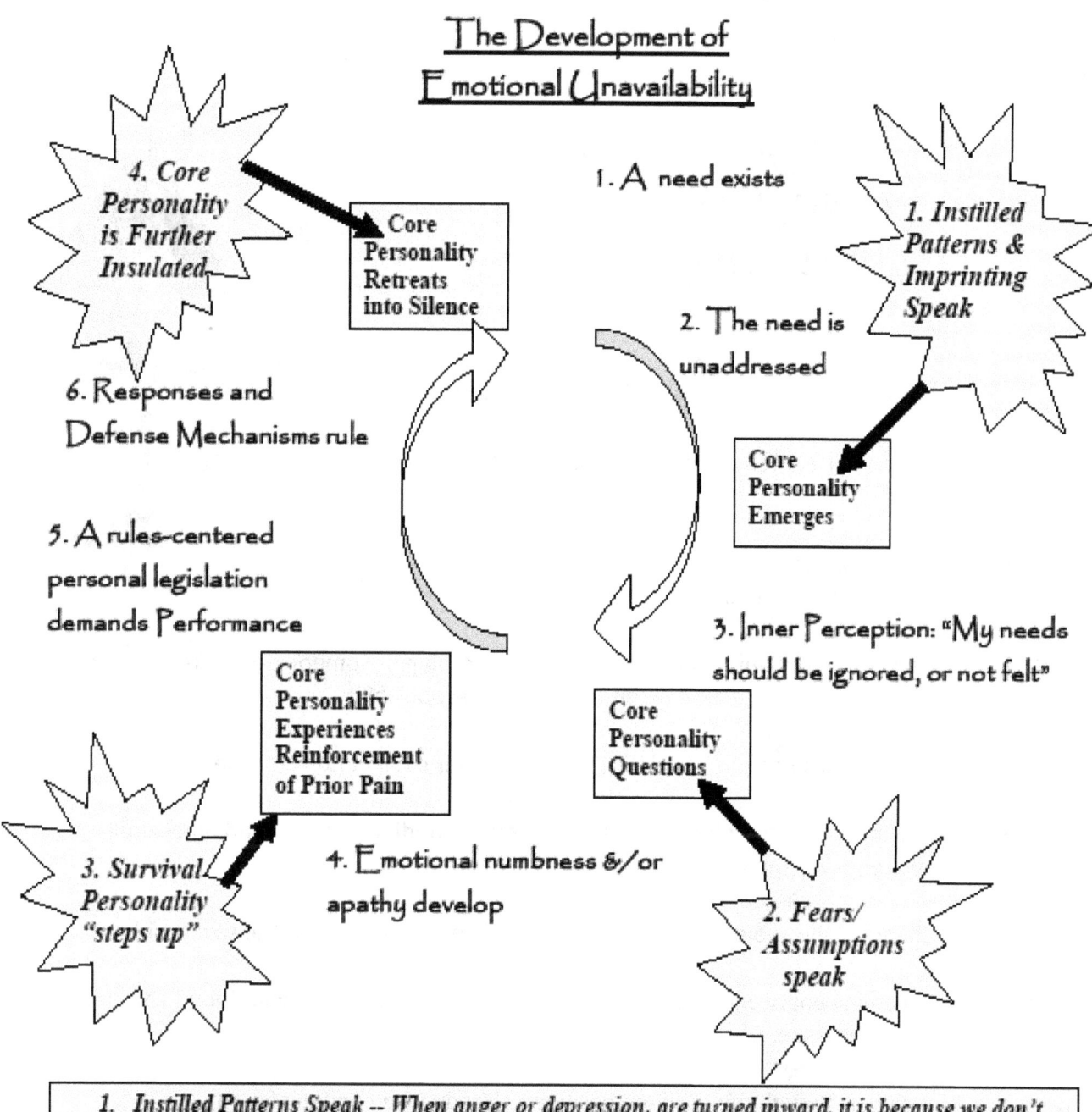

1. **Instilled Patterns Speak** -- When anger or depression, are turned inward, it is because we don't want to assess the damage inside of our souls. It is denial/avoidance.
2. **Fears/Assumptions Speak** --We become angry at ourselves, or punish ourselves for: a) having a need, b) being weak, c) being afraid, d) being "selfish", e) making a mistake; doing/saying the wrong thing.
3. **Survival Personality "steps up"** – We tell ourselves "I don't need it anyway," or "I'll try harder to push through." We take on the attributes of those who hurt us, by trying to "become" the one who was stronger than we were.
4. **Core Personality is Further Insulated** – This pattern creates another layer of insulation upon the ability to sense and feel anything except the strongest negative emotions – (fear, anger, rage, depression, etc.) When even these emotions are deemed unacceptable, the soul retreats, and waits for intentional development.

© dcg/atg

Most (if not all) Addicts & Codependents Live in a State of Denial

Denial is the second step in the Steps of Grief:

- Pretending something does not exists when in reality it does

- Being willing to admit there is a problem, but unwilling to see the severity of it

- Seeing the problem as being caused by something or someone else. The behavior is not denied, but its cause is someone else's responsibility.

- Offering excuses, alibis, justifications and other explanations for the behavior

- Dealing with the problem on a general level; avoiding personal and emotional awareness of the situations or conditions

- Changing the subject to avoid topics that threaten to address the real problem

- Becoming angry and irritable when reference is made to the condition. This helps to avoid the issue.

- Acting as though the problem has been already faced and dealt with.

- Never resolving conflict – just letting it settle; then acting as though nothing happened at all.

The Steps of Grief

Over the past thirty years or so, I have had the opportunity to help many people, and see healing come to a spectrum of addiction/codependency issues. Without exception, in my experience, the problem of addiction has manifested during a person's experience with Loss of one form or another. Over the years, the seven Steps of Grief in the chart on the next page have repeated themselves over and over again. Here is an explanation of those steps:

As a catalyst for the grieving process to begin, an incident occurs: whether an abuse, a molestation, a trauma, a death, or an injury of one kind or another. At that point, the steps begin.

Step One.   **Shock.**   *The person feels numb, and is unable to connect with what has happened. They cannot communicate, and many times are in a mental fog. Some traumatic events are blocked out.*

Step Two.   **Denial.**   *The person builds an image of what they wish would happen, or what an acceptable form of Life or a circumstance would look like. I call this a "Denial Bubble." The person then defends and protects that image with one or any combination of defense mechanisms. Defense mechanisms have the ability to distract the emotions, and many times even relationships in the person's life, preventing the admission and processing of what has really happened. In many instances, a person will surround themselves with people who will confirm their denial efforts, even rejecting those who remind them of the Truth of their reality.*

Step Three.   **Hurt.**   *To some extent, whether in surface or in depth, the person begins To move past Denial, into deeper areas of emotional experience. The Reality of the event is admitted (whether partially or completely), and the person begins to sense Hurt and inward Pain.*

Step Four.   **Anger.**   *As Pain deepens, the person comes to grips with the injustice of the traumatic event they have suffered. In its pure form, Anger is actually an empowerment to help the person move forward, making positive changes. (For a more complete discussion of Anger, please see "A Christian Counselor's Primer on Anger -- Book One by Debbye Graafsma.)*

Step Five. **Depression.** As Anger fades, or proves to be ineffective in providing the change needed, the person is left with the Truth of their personal Reality. If the person has not dealt properly with their Anger, (allowing Hurt to be disclosed and processed for healing), then the Anger is many times turned inward. This is one form of Depression, however.

Step Six. **Acceptance.** When a person begins to move from Depression to Acceptance, they become aware of the differences between their "Denial Bubble," (their former concept of Reality), and their present Reality. The distance in difference between the two extremes will determine the depth of the person's Depression.

Step Seven. **Resolution & Growth.** The person does the hard work of bringing together what they thought Life should look like (the "Denial Bubble"), and their present Reality. They make the decision to stop comparing the unattainable with the present, and find themselves able to chart a path to move forward into Health and Healing.

"Denial separates the mind from the agony of the heart. A wall of denial is maintained only by the use of costly energies."
Wilson

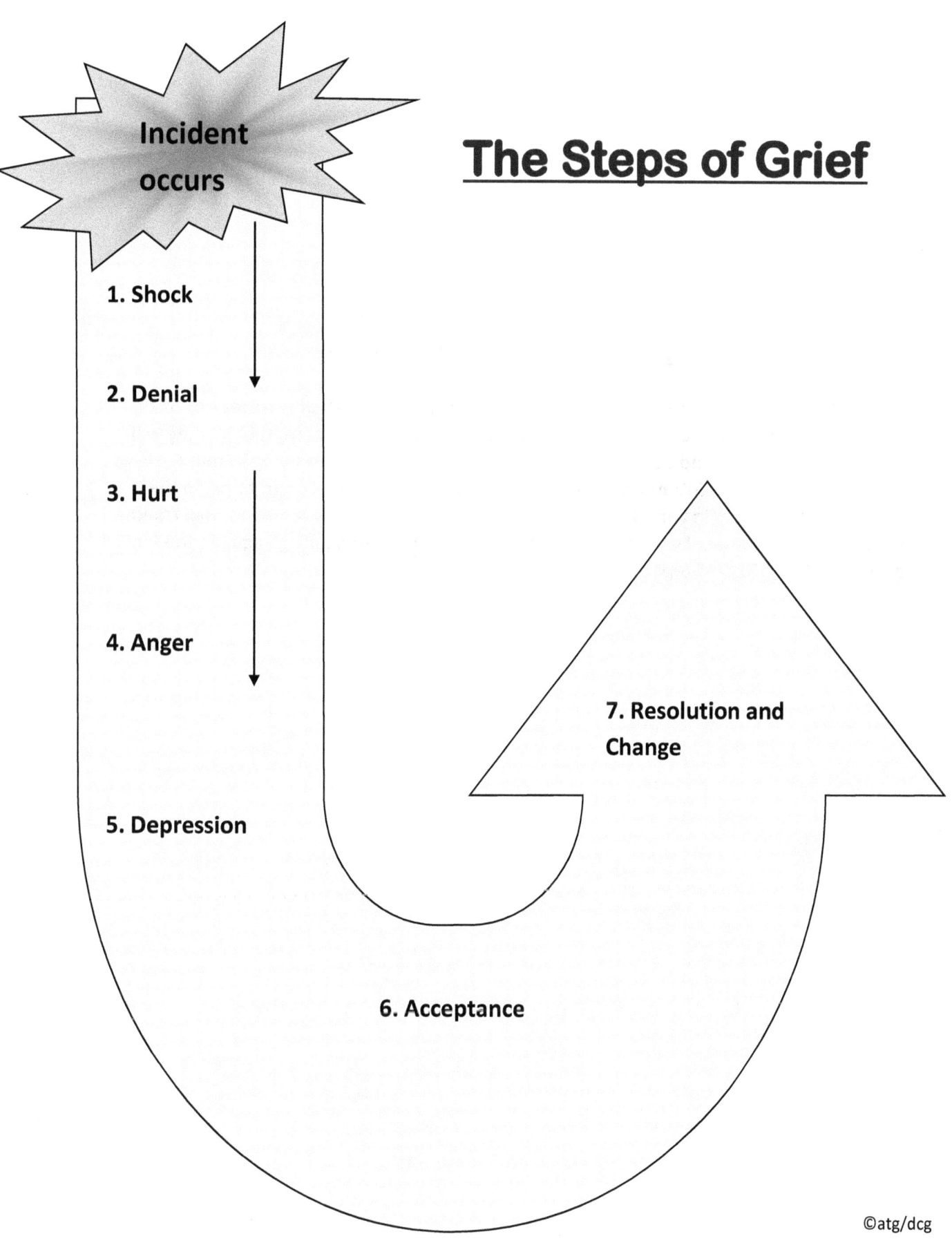

Cycles of Stalled Grief – (chart, page 51)

When a person experiences an inability to walk through all of the Steps of Grief, usually determining that one form or another in the journey is "unacceptable," they will "bounce" off of a step and begin to cycle. The person then continues living in that Cycle of Stalled Grief, until they intentionally address the Pain which caused them to begin the grieving process to begin with. Cycling patterns can be reinforced when additional trauma occurs in a person's life. Unprocessed grief can do a sort of "stockpiling" against the feared (or resisted) step in the Steps of Grief.

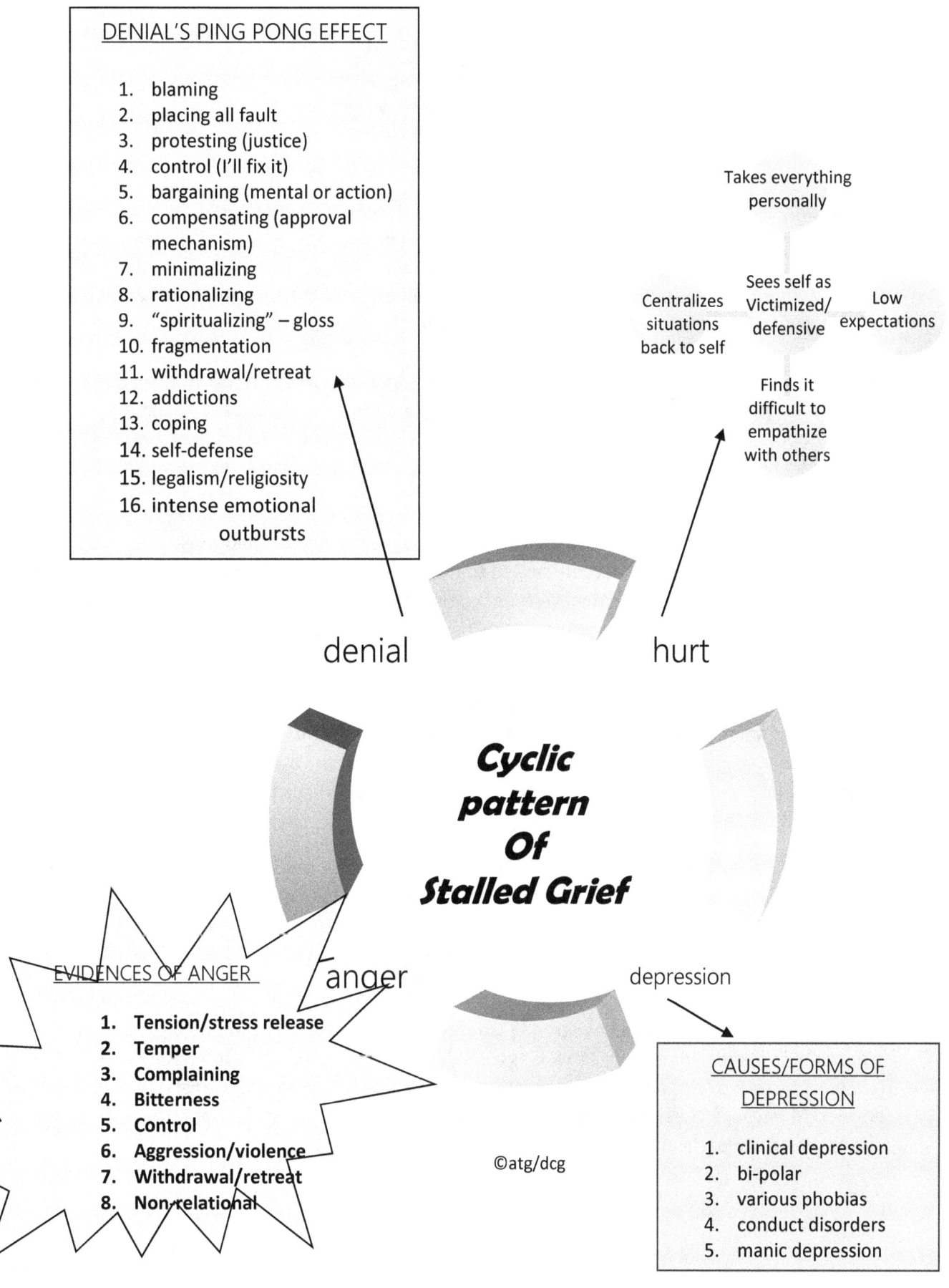

Grieving... What?

*He is despised and rejected of men; a man of sorrows,
and acquainted with grief: and we hid as it were
our faces from him; he was despised, and we esteemed him not." Is 53:4*

Grief is part of the human condition. We are each in different stages of grief, in at least one area of living. And, because grief carries pain, it is part of our nature to avoid it, deny it, and many times stockpile it, putting off the process of dealing with it. And then, inevitably, when the growth process has been delayed, it builds into an emotional tsunami; overwhelming and debilitating; sabotaging our joy, diminishing our effectiveness, distracting our focus.

Everyone on the planet experiences loss. Loss comes in many different forms; from the loss of a person's hopes and dreams, to the loss of a family member through death, rejection, circumstances or divorce. The classic author, C.S. Lewis, once said, "No one ever told me that grief felt so like fear." In my own loss experiences, grief has come in waves, unexpectedly, when I least expected it.

In the case of Addictions and Codependency, grief is a greater factor than those who are touched by it realize.   As we have discussed to this point, most people who deal with addiction are self-medicating, in order to deal with pain, grief, and loss. Additionally, many codependents find themselves compensating for losses they have experienced, by becoming performance oriented, taking control, and seeking to earn love and approval.

Sometimes, the issues flow from a person's family of origin; the nest of our childhood. Weak attachments and damaged bonding experiences with our authority figures can cause us to develop areas of broken trust, finding it difficult to trust others. Or, in cases of neglect, the ability to relate to others is ignored in our development, causing us to become adults who do not understand the value of relationships.

But there is even more to the Grief problem. Unaware, we are each born already grieving the condition of our human spirit. Because of man's choice to sin in Eden, our innate desire for a happy and perfect life is short-circuited by the factor of Sin. The Bible teaches us that until we experience redemption, our human spirit is dead. When surrender to Christ's gift of Life occurs, the human spirit is born again into the spiritual realm, making us eternally alive.

To help give understanding in how greatly Grief adversely impacts our ability to grow into emotionally healthy adulthood; serving as a catalyst for many difficulties in relational living; the following page provides a charted description of human bonding needs, the relational ability developed because of each particular emotional need being met through bonding, and the age during which the particular need for attachment is most vulnerable.

Human Core Desires

IQ (head, intellect)

1. Cliches   (to be "normal")   To be acknowledged (complimented, praised)
                                         To be noticed (seen)

2. Facts   (to "matter")   To be seen (recognized, remembered)
                                         To be physically safe
                                         To be included
                                         To be affirmed

> Achievement, Task, and Image-based.

EQ (emotions and sense of self)

3. Values, Principles (male)   To experience safe touch
       Morals and Feelings (female)   To be heard
                                           To belong
          (to be "in the group")   To be received

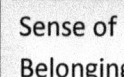

4. Needs and Yearnings   To be emotionally safe (and secure)
       (to be "at home in all   To be chosen ("first pick for the team")
          Settings")   To be understood (sense of connection)
                                         To be included
                                         To be trusted

> Sense of Belonging
>
> And Sense of Being

---

5. **Inner Child -- Core Union**
          To be chosen (worth waiting for)
          (usually within marriage – can be a   To be safe (without fear, no need to hide)
          David/Jonathan relationship)   To be trusted completely (no sense of rejection
                                                                           or disapproval)

          to have something unique
          to offer/ to serve well)

We cannot give away what we have never received.

It is helpful to help a client take apart life history and levels of relationship experienced in the bonding processes from the family of origin. Understanding a person's survival mechanisms, based upon their family relationships, can aid discovery and growth in development.

Family Diagrams

*Note: Father God's plan and purpose for family life is a safe and secure place; emotionally, physically, and spiritually for each family member. Family Life is a God-created environment where Design and Destiny can be discovered, encouraged, developed and pursued with purpose. While Marriage is a Place **where intimate relationship is developed** between a man and woman who have chosen each other for a life partnership, Family Life is a place **where the children are to be developed** and allowed to grow, encouraged by the parents.*

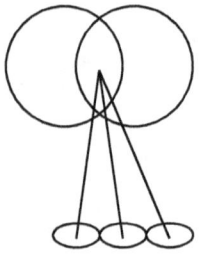

Healthy Family

Father and Mother have learned to operate together, and present decisions and options to children together, as a unified team. Children are ministered to on an equal basis, with no favoritism shown or expressed. **Focus: Abba's plan for the common good.**

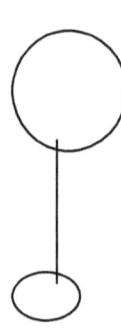

Healthy Single Parent Relationship

Each parent has learned to connect with the child's inner person, and can communicate from a relational point of view future goals and discipline.

Focus: Abba's plan for the common good.

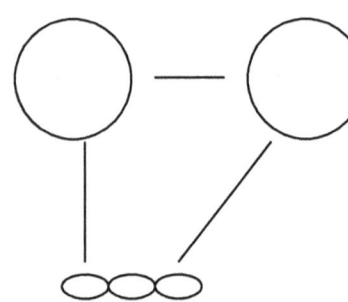

Unhealthy Parent Relationships

Parents are unconnected with each other and with the children. Communication takes place regarding task and fact levels only. Children receive communication, but there is no connection. Result: children receive a sense of abandonment and isolation, and become task oriented for approval. There is little or no affection communicated.
Focus: Personal rights, needs and/or appetites.

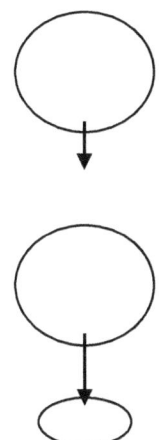

Authority Driven Model (unhealthy)

One parent is seen as having all authority, and communicates with the children through a chain-of-command, without personal relationship with the child. The child is distanced in the relationship and has no opportunity to appeal or question decisions. Voice and Identity are diminished within the family, for all members except the family member with the most authority.

Also within this model, one parent must continually explain the other to the child. The parent in the explaining role tends to lose personal identity and become co-dependent, seeking to keep peace in the home at any price. Acceptance is performance oriented.
Focus: To succeed on all fronts. To meet expectations

The Abuse Model

The parents have experienced relational failure in their own abilities to build a marriage. They are emotionally distanced. Communication regarding the relationship is made to the child, and the child feels they must choose between parents.

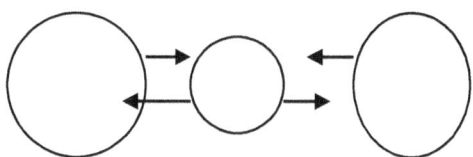

The child becomes the caretaker, and must meet the emotional needs of the parent; many times this involves verbal, emotional, physical, or sexual abuse (order of progression). The child must continually choose between parents, and perceives they must keep everyone happy. Identity development is stopped, and the child must choose an alternate "power" personality to survive. If a "power" personality is not found, the child will become depressed and lethargic. Approval is shame based
Focus: To survive

The Island Model

The parents have experienced relational failure in their own abilities to build a marriage. They are emotionally distanced. There is no communication.

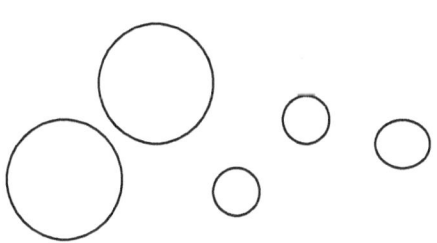

Everyone in the family lives in a separate environment. Everyone Is taking care of themselves, and no one is connected emotionally.

There Is no care on mutual level.
There are no bonding moments that can be remembered in this model
Focus: To survive

Bonding, Attachment, Morality and Conscience Development

In the past 15 years, studies done by many groups in the human development and counseling fields, have shown that a person's emotional health and development is directly responsible for many things. Here is the short list:

1. *The ability to feel and label emotions.*
2. *The ability to empathize with other people.*
3. *The desire to do the right thing, gaining approval (conscience).*
4. *The ability to relate and interconnect in relationship.*
5. *Character development.*
6. *The ability to maintain long-term relationships.*

Many addictions and codependent behaviors can be traced to the detached sense of "being outside the circle," or "being different," felt by those who have experienced damaged attachments during development years.

On the following page is a chart, contrasting the stages of emotional bonding. The chart is designed to show thought mechanisms and emotional needs of persons who have not experienced healthy bonding, and are therefore fear-driven in the left hand column. In the center, is a description of the needs of persons who have impaired bonding/damaged attachments. Finally, in the right hand column is a description of a person with healthy bonding patterns, who has learned to live in confidence, without addictions or codependency; who has healthy bonding abilities in relationship.

I find it is helpful to have a client study the chart, and mark the thinking patterns they recognize in the columns. This can help to pinpoint struggles the client is currently facing in their relational abilities.

Levels of Attachment and Conscience Development

Unbonded Unattached	Fragile Or untooled in Bonding	Incomplete Or fractional Bonding	Damaged Or weakened Attachment	Standard or Normal Bonding	Well-Bonded and Attached
Serial Killers Sexual Violence (for pleasure)	Criminals Thieves Prostitutes	Thrill-seekers Some Spies "Danger" addicts	"Charmers," slick presenters, some politicians, "The show must continue mindset"	Intact & well-adjusted families/healthy relationships	Humanitarians Those who give their lives for others
Sociopaths Psychopaths (Ted Bundy) (Charles Mansen) (Adolph Hitler)		---- Narcissists (ego-driven) ---- Prima Donnas			Philanthropists Missionaries (Teresa of Calcutta) (Albert Schweitzer)

FEAR Driven ⇅ **LOVE Led**

Unattached: Unbonded
Dulled: Evil Conscience

- Un-motivated
- Taker from others
- Wrong moral choices
- Critical, laughs at other's pain
- Manipulation, "con"
- Rejects relationship
- Feels nothing
- Stubborn, has no need
- Silent, stoic
- Refuses Truth, alternates own view
- Negative flow
- No hope or future
- Violence
- Closed, impassive
- Bloody images, death

Attachment Disorders
Impaired Conscience

- motivated by gain
- non-contributor
- passive
- laughs at others
- dishonesty, charmer
- hiding in group, loner
- feels negative emotion
- argumentative, debating
- responds only
- argues with Truth
- sporadic flow
- half-empty perspective
- sarcasm, anger
- narcissist in heart, abusive
- abnormal fears, depressed

Healthy Attachment
Healthy Conscience

- self-disciplines evident
- giving to others
- solid moral choices
- sense of humor, laughs at self
- honesty
- ability to relate
- ability to feel and process emotion
- teachable
- has an ability to communicate
- Understands and applies Truth
- creative flow
- half-full perspective
- gentleness
- openness of heart
- normal fears

Note: *All addicts and codependents struggle with elements of Shame.*

Toxic Shame
Which methods of coping seem familiar to you?

Deep, unhealthy shame is the internal feeling that we are "dirty", flawed as a person, or not good enough. When we have always lived with a sense of underlying shame, we may believe these feelings are normal, and may think all other people feel the same way. When we allow this mindset to infect our approach to relationships, it stops us from experiencing the love and Presence of God.

Toxic shame says things like:

> *"I'm a failure"* …. *"Nobody could possibly love me*
> *"I'm no good at anything* …. *"I can't relate to other people"*

Coping Mechanisms:

Self-Abuse: Hurting or contemplating hurting yourself whether in thought or with bodily action.
Chronic Victimization: Feeling used. Not recognizing, or taking care of personal needs; not believing you have the right to say "no;" Blaming others for your life situations and the consequences of those choices.
Abuse of Others: taking out unresolved hurt and anger on others who are more helpless (like hitting, kicking or throwing; even yelling; or becoming emotionally unavailable)
Depression: being weighed down by heavy feelings of hopelessness, powerlessness, and a sense of being overwhelmed.
Rage: the unleashing of anger in order to keep other people away, whether consciously or subconsciously. Rage is the expression of a feeling of powerlessness and being controlled. The act of intimidating others creates a false sense of safety in the mind.
Control: Taking power in a situation. This is done to minimize the fear of vulnerability in the life. Shame fears being vulnerable due to potential rejection.
Perfectionism: Unrealistic expectations, fear of being abandoned if we're not good, right, perfect, constantly keeping unreasonable standards of practice and behavior.
Addictions and other Compulsions: shame is at the heart of all addictions/compulsions. Shame sets a person up for psychological dependency which can lead to physical dependency.
> Compulsive relationships – looking for others to fill us up.
> Enmeshed relationships – primary goal is passions and excitement.
> Apathetic relationships – primary goal is avoiding vulnerability and pain. Each person walks down a parallel track with physical, emotional and sometimes social distance between them.

Suicide/attempts: Shame convinces the person they have nothing to live for, that they are hopeless, unworthy and don't deserve or want to live.

Note: *All addicts are narcissistic; believing they should be treated as the center of the life orbit of those around them. The first addiction is that of being addicted to Self. That would means one's own appetites, opinions and emotions. Substance or behavior driven addictions are secondary addictions, and are fed by narcissism at the core of the personality.*

Narcissistic Personality Disorder (NPD)
How to Recognize a Narcissist

1. **All Addicts are narcissists; their opinions, needs, attitudes, emotions, and appetites must be considered first.**

2. **All Codependents are addicted to keeping their addict "happy."**

3. **This sick see-saw plays out the cyclic drama of Addiction and Codependency.**

On a biblical level, to be a narcissist is to be a lover of self. People who have NPD, are then, those described in II Timothy 3:1-2, as those who live in the last days, putting themselves and their own desires above everything else. These are difficult people indeed.

We all have had to deal with difficult people, many in ongoing high-maintenance relationships. Some days we can even be pretty difficult ourselves. Recognizing the difference between normal difficulties and personality disorders can be crucial to decisions about entering new relationships and continuing existing relationships. Be aware as you work through these materials, that most people who have come to the point where self-love has become an emotional disorder, have ingrained the behavior. Most clinical materials tend to describe narcissists as unwilling, rather than unable to change. For change to take place, the person must admit to Pride motivations, and humble themselves, seeking true repentance and humility before God.

Self-love, or Narcissism can manifest itself in many different ways

A Narcissist:

* Is always right, and other people are always wrong. Those in relationship with a narcissist learn to distrust their own judgment, and, as a by-product, learn to practice shame; they are never good enough to gain the narcissist's agreement.

* Can never be pleased completely. They are extremely sensitive, and somewhat unaccepting of personal criticism, but they are overly critical of others.
* Has a grandiose mindset of their own importance.

- Has a difficult time maintaining close personal relationships without making demands.

- Is better at lying than they are at telling the truth. They have an immature conscience, and usually stay inside the boundaries given because they are afraid of losing their reputation, or because they are afraid of punishment.

- Is given to wildly misinterpreting the speech and actions of others

- Thinks in pervasive patterns of fantasy, and have a great need for admiration.

- Lacks empathy for others; and the pain and/or needs of others. They "tune out" when the needs or pains of others are expressed. They actually have a short circuit in regard to the ability to connect with other people's pain, yet they expect their own pain to be given first consideration when it occurs.

- Refuses to change their behavior, even when it harms, or causes emotional distress, disturbing others.

- Has difficulty handling disagreement. They will respond in one of two extremes. They will attack, or they will withdraw.

- Expects to be honored and recognized as superior for their achievements, even when those achievements do not deserve accolades or awards of merit. Self-importance exaggerates the importance of their contribution to the group.

- Wants to be treated as if they are the only one in the picture. They belittle and complain about the efforts of others, often expressing that they have sacrificed more than anyone else.

- Has aspirations and ambitions much larger than their evident talents; "full of themselves."

- Practices a preoccupation with fantasies of unlimited success, power, brilliance, beauty, or ideal love (they live in their "own little world")

- Is impulsive

- Believes he or she is "special" and can only be understood by, or should associate with, other special or high-status people (or institutions). Narcissists think that everyone who is not special and superior is worthless. By definition, normal, ordinary, and average people aren't special and superior, and so, to narcissists, they are worthless. (This disorder rates people according to their importance and significance, believes God does too, when the person acknowledges God's authority). *Note: When a person truly turns to Jesus, there is a change of heart, and the person becomes focused upon obedience and submission to the Spirit of God. The life purpose of a Christian, then, is to become like Christ, and not to satisfy their own appetites and desires. In most regards, a Narcissist has set their own desires above their own need for the Presence of God to rule and lead the life.*

- Requires excessive admiration and attention, even deference. Frequency and volume are more important to this person than sincerity.

- Feels the need to keep up an image, or live up to pretensions.

- Carries a sense of entitlement, meaning that they expect automatic compliance with their wishes, desiring especially favorable treatment. For example, thinking they should always be able to go first and that other people should stop whatever they're doing to do what the narcissists want. A narcissist may react with hurt or rage when these expectations are frustrated.

- Will selfishly take advantage of others to achieve their own ends, meaning they will use other people to get what they want, without really caring about the cost to other people.

- Is often envious of others or believes that others are envious of him. They are competitive in unusual ways, and offended easily.

- Shows arrogant, haughty, patronizing, or contemptuous behaviors or attitudes. They treat other people badly, and are numb to the fact they have done it. "Blindness" of heart and mind.

- Does not respond well when asked to "have a heart," or asked to make amends. The response tends to be defensiveness, and asking them to make an apology can usually make matters worse in the relationship.

- Can contradict themselves, sometimes in the same sentence.

- Tend to be disappointing gift givers. However, when buying for themselves, they feel the need to purchase designer labels, name brand items, because it comforts them, and serves as a symbol of authority for their choices and tastes. Most narcissists are insecure about their personal taste, and allow themselves to copy those close to them, or those they admire, in purchasing clothing, or personal items.

- Has difficulty following a mutual theme of discussion. A narcissist has difficulty connecting with the message being communicated by the other person, and although they hear the words, they have problems being able to understand what will affect them, or how their actions affect others. In these situations, they overlook the fact that other people will react negatively to them, and don't understand the trouble their actions cause to others.

- Considers their needs of utmost importance, and as a practice, demand that those needs be met, sometimes with anger, abuse, or pouting and manipulation.

- Desires to be the center of attention in most gatherings, or situations. If they are not the center of attention, the narcissist tends to withdraw.

- Has difficulty admitting or recognizing their own feelings.

- Will give a person a gift that they know the person doesn't really want, especially if the item is something with a low cost.

- As a normal rule, narcissists don't want to change -- they want the world to change. As a practice, they criticize, gripe, and complain about almost everything and almost everyone almost all the time.

- Tends to be passive in life approach and vulnerable, even though their response to relationships around them tend to be ferocious and accusing.

- Tends to be negative, pessimistic, or gloomy most of the time.

- Lacks a sense of humor. They don't really "get" jokes, but confuse sarcasm for humor, usually at another person's expense.

- Is completely and without exception authority based. In other words, they desire to be authority figures and, short of that, they want to be associated with authority figures

- Is very difficult to spend simple, uncomplicated time with.

- Can be secretive or perhaps unusually reserved or very jealous of their privacy

Some personality traits of the Narcissist can be compared to those of a healthy six year old child, which might possibly indicate emotional crippling in childhood in those who struggle with these tendencies.

Some of those traits include, but are not limited to:

amoral/conscienceless	authoritarian
care only about appearances	contemptuous
critical of others	cruel
disappointing gift-givers	don't recognize own feelings
envious and competitive	feel entitled
flirtatious or seductive	grandiose
hard to have a good time with	hate to live alone
hyper-sensitive to criticism	impulsive
lack sense of humor	naive
passive	pessimistic
religious	secretive
self-contradictory	stingy
strange work habits	unusual eating habits
weird sense of time	craves center of attention

Narcissism is a long-term pattern of abnormal thinking, feeling, and behavior in many different situations. Contact with narcissists may make you feel bad about yourself. In the workplace, many times a narcissist will have a history of alienating colleagues, co-workers, employees, students, clients, and customers, although most Narcissists are high functioning, and hold levels of responsibility.

Narcissism is a short circuiting of a person's understanding of personal identity, as well as a misunderstanding of how that identity fits within relationship and community. The disorder can be caused by over-indulgent parents, who train a child that their viewpoint and desires should always be honored above all. The disorder can also be caused by instability in family history, abandonment and abuse, where the child is left to their own devices, and must find their own way.

The narcissist's path, therefore, becomes the only "right way" for the grown adult to live, and teachability becomes an absent quality in the life. To grow and change out of narcissism requires humility and intentional selflessness, and the choosing to serve others. This, however, can become over-balanced if done in the person's own efforts, without the guidance of the Holy Spirit; the end result of which will be Codependency.

Narcissism promotes the attributes of denial, as the person's right of defense. It can be the underlying cause of depressions, and addictions, as well as compulsive behaviors.

If and when a Narcissist enters treatment (because it is miracle for them to admit when they are wrong) it is a rare event. When a narcissist does enter treatment, they progress very slowly, because every point has to be proved and debated before it is accepted as factual truth.

Clinical Descriptions:

Mild impairment when self-centered or egotistical behavior results in occasional minor problems, but the person is generally doing pretty well.

Moderate impairment when self-centered or egotistical behavior results in:
(a) missing days from work, household duties, or school,
(b) significant performance problems as a wage-earner, homemaker, or student,
(c) frequently avoiding or alienating friends,
(d) significant risk of harming self or others (frequent suicidal preoccupation; often neglecting family, or frequently abusing others or committing criminal acts).

Severe impairment when self-centered or egotistical behavior results in:
(a) staying in bed all day,
(b) totally alienating all friends and family,
(c) severe risk of harming self or others (failing to maintain personal hygiene; persistent danger of suicide, abuse, or crime).

How many narcissists does it take to change a light bulb?
(a) Just one -- but he has to wait for the whole world to revolve around him.
(b) None at all -- he hires menials for work that's beneath him.

Addiction and Narcissism

1. An addict is a with-holder when it comes to love relationships – what that means –

2. An addict will always hold to the beliefs of narcissism – and argue about whether what they do is really wrong – how could it hurt them or others when its really helping them— people just don't understand, etc.

3. We are our own most important core value, we will become lovers of self, more than we are lovers of God – this means we will abuse our relationships, and we will abuse others.

4. Addicts are always abusers – first of themselves, then of others.

Am *I* codependent?

One of the main questions I ask clients who I suspect might deal with codependency is: "What do you do for fun?" Most codependent people realize they feel consistently unfulfilled in their relationships. Most have difficulty expressing or admitting when they have a need, and find it difficult to receive care from others without feeling obligated to reciprocate. Most feel overloaded and many deal with stress related diseases.

Codependents have difficulty with areas of intimacy—of knowing and being known, and tend to take a long time to trust others. Since many codependents were raised by narcissistic, addicted or emotionally un-tooled parents, perfectionism presents itself as a force to be reckoned with on a regular basis. This fear-based behavior is most often interpreted by others as controlling behavior. Compounded by all of these symptoms, most codependents try to anticipate threats of danger, and expect others to feel what they feel.

But that sounds like problems everyone deals with.

There are several difficulties in helping a person discover a need for freedom from codependency. When a child requires extra care, such as is the case for a medically fragile child, the behavior displayed by the parents could be misunderstood as codependent. However, the necessity of that type of caregiving is far from codependent. In our culture, we are taught to avoid conflict; to be "nice;" to be independent; to keep our opinions to ourselves. These unspoken cultural "rules" tend to encourage the development of codependency in relationships, rather than a healthy and mutual interdependence.

In my own journey, I have come to the belief that all persons without the Life of the Holy Spirit of God at the core of their personal life orbit are addicts. And, when confronted with a need for change, most of us have simply changed one addiction for another. We allow what we do, to bring fulfillment to us, defining our purpose. God's intention, however, is that we find fulfillment in our relationship with Him, and allow Him to define our purpose. In this way, addiction and codependency are both actually a struggle with personal idolatry. In other words, the center stage position of our lives has been tampered with. We have replaced God with something or someone. We may have even placed ourselves in the center. And, whatever is place on the stage in the center of our life orbit has our full attention. Our attitudes and responses rotate around the success or failure of that focus point to make us happy. In a sense, we worship whatever we have allowed to take that center stage spot in our lives.

That being said, then …. What are we allowing ourselves to worship?

Where does codependency come from? Why does it happen?

Over the years, it has become a generally held belief that codependency is learned in our family nest system during developmental years. The cultural rules of that nest system have developed over time, and patterns of behavior and thinking are passed down from one generation to another. When rejection, ridicule, or disapproval occur, shaming or embarrassing a member (usually an adult) in the nest system, the rules are reinforced, and behaviors are enacted to protect the reputation and image of the other nest system members. When the rules are enforced, members of the nest system (usually the children and subservient members) will feel alienated from outside relationships, and isolated from activities not common to the group.

There are two most common rules in nest systems, or families, with this structure.

They are:
1. "Don't show"   *meaning*   Family members are not to expose negative opinions or emotions, to anyone outside of the system.

2. "Don't tell"   *meaning*   Family members are not to discuss weaknesses, addictions, or problems with anyone outside of the system.

Additionally, conflict is avoided. To prevent conflict, the family adopts other behaviors to reinforce the basic two rules. These include: "Keep your feelings to yourself;" "Never make waves;" "Always be the best;" "Never think of yourself, even when it comes to your health," "Ignore the example, and do as you are told," "Don't draw attention to yourself," "Never be silly or have too much fun." When conflict is "felt" in the midst of family relationships, members will speak to a third party rather than directly to each other.

Conversely, when a nest system is healthy:

- Conflict is discussed and problems are resolved as a team
- Communication is open and honest
- Doing one's best is good enough
- Effort is respected and appreciated
- What you see is what you get
- Each person is allowed to make discoveries and explore creativity

In an Addicted/Codependent family, the absence of a healthy environment presents a void. That void is filled with the rules and silent tension of a narcissistic orbit and frustrated family members. Coping becomes a way of life, with emotional constriction as a support system for the perfect image. Those within the family have no concept of their personal value, their true identity, or their purpose. Many family members in this type of family nest have so adapted and adjusted their personalities to survive living with day-to-day dysfunction.

What is the best way to change the pattern?

There are several condition indicators common to all codependents. Most codependents struggle with being assertive, and with active listening. All have areas of living in which they can only maintain their personal sense of safety and confidence by wielding and holding control. In my own counseling practice, I begin with assertiveness training; helping a client discover get in touch with their true deep emotions and voice them. From there assertiveness training comes easily, while keeping an eye on the levels of control being exercised by the person. Remember, Life Patterns cannot change overnight. And, a person can only handle one side of a situation at a time. Slow gains in growth tend to be permanent, while quick change is fleeting. Never be afraid to speak truth to a client, but remember to take one inch at a time, rather than expect more than your client can achieve.

__Note:__ When counseling a codependent person, a therapist must be vigilant in maintaining personal boundaries; not succumbing to temptation to their own codependent, caregiving weaknesses.

How Does Co-Dependency Begin in a Person's Life?

In order for a person to develop and grow in a healthy manner, there are four elements of personhood which need to be present and communicated during development. When any leg of the "stool" is missing, or allowed to be "too short, or uneven," in the life, a child will grow up with specific gaps in their awareness of what healthy Personhood looks like. They will find it difficult to interact and maintain relationships with others, without personal criteria.

Elements of Personhood:

1. Voice – any expression of the inner self

2. Community – the sense that I am part of a larger picture than myself; that I fit within that group

3. Relationship – specific and intentional emotional attachments in which I am mutually committed to growth and connection on an ongoing basis.

4. Empowerment – the confidence and ability to express inner and outer life processes: the power to live an honest portrayal of inner motivations.

To more thoroughly assess a client's personal life approach, the **G.E.M.S. Personal Assessment Tool** *by Debbye Graafsma will provide a more comprehensive viewpoint. The tool is available on lulu.com and on amazon.com. For audio teaching sessions accompanying the tool, please contact us through our website at awakenedtogrow.com.*

Charts for Further Resourcing

The Effects of Chemical Substances on the Brain

Sequential damage upon neural tissue

1. The frontal part of the brain is affected impairing the ability to make decisions and control of motor skills/coordination.

2. The middle inner part of the brain is affected, causing loss of emotional control, and the potential loss of consciousness.

3. The Cerebellum and Brain Stem are affected, causing a deregulation of body temperature, heart rate, appetite and conscious awareness. At this effect level, the risk of death is extremely high.

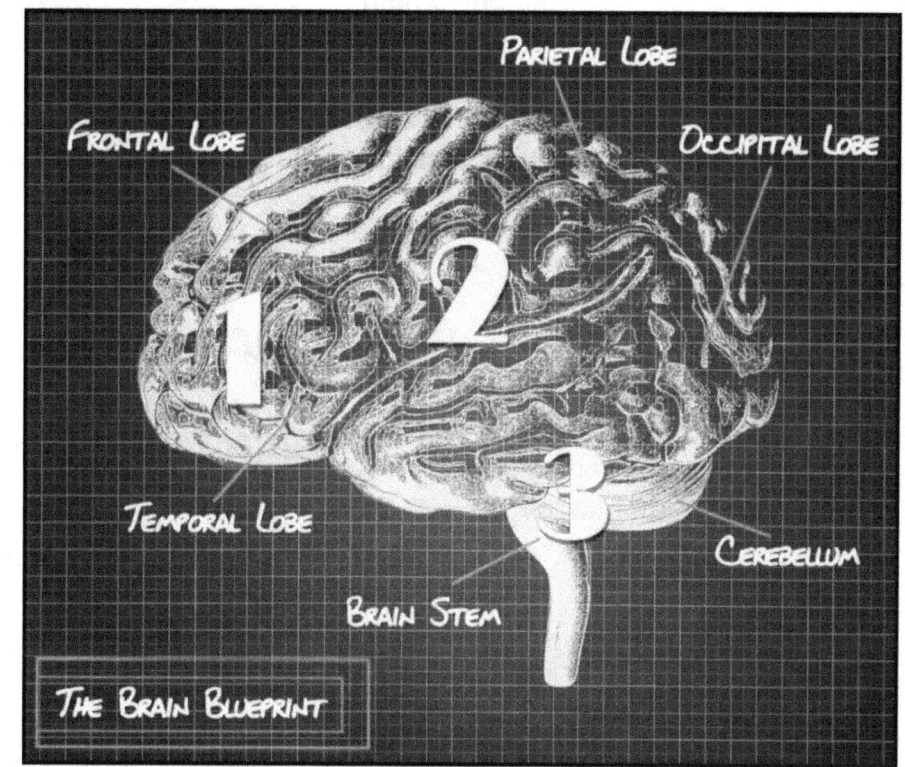

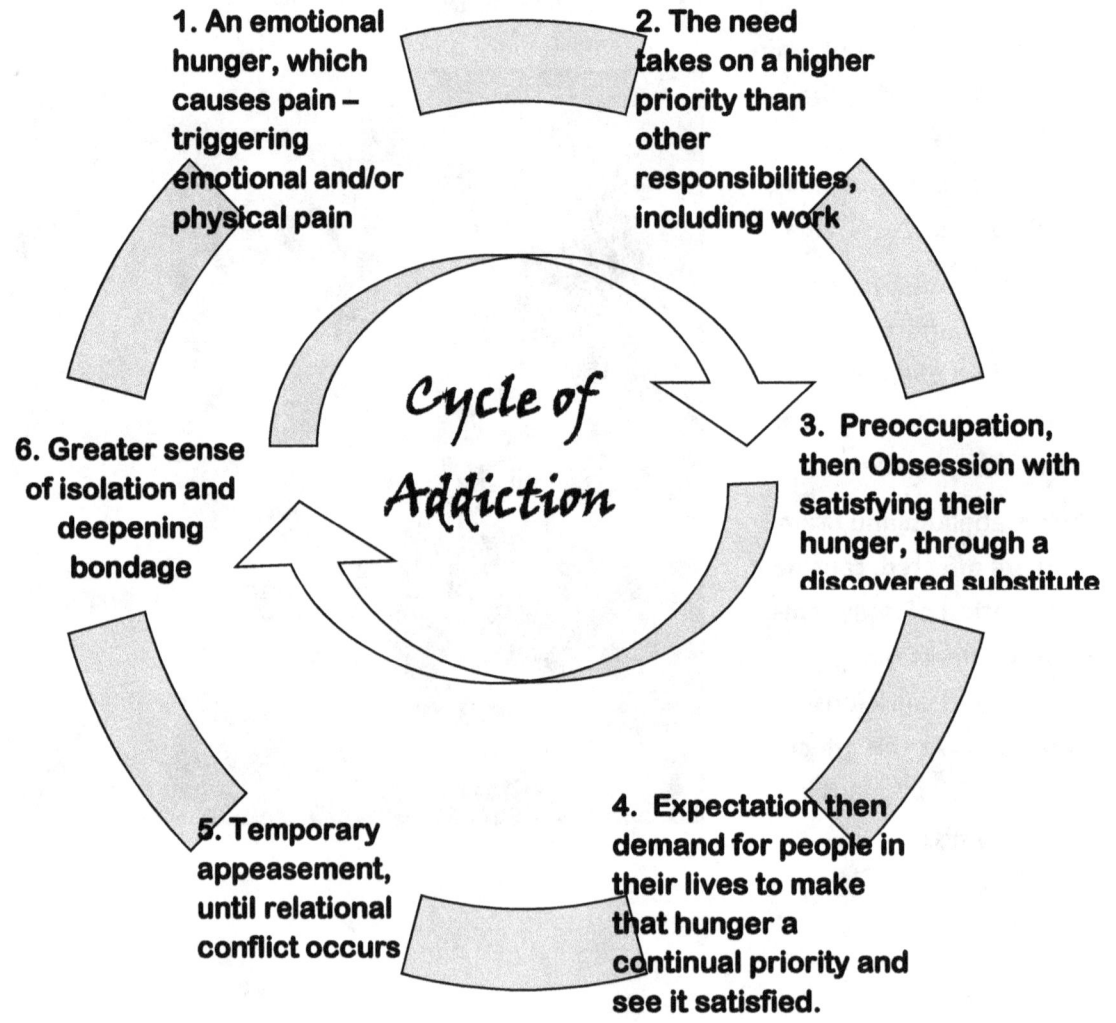

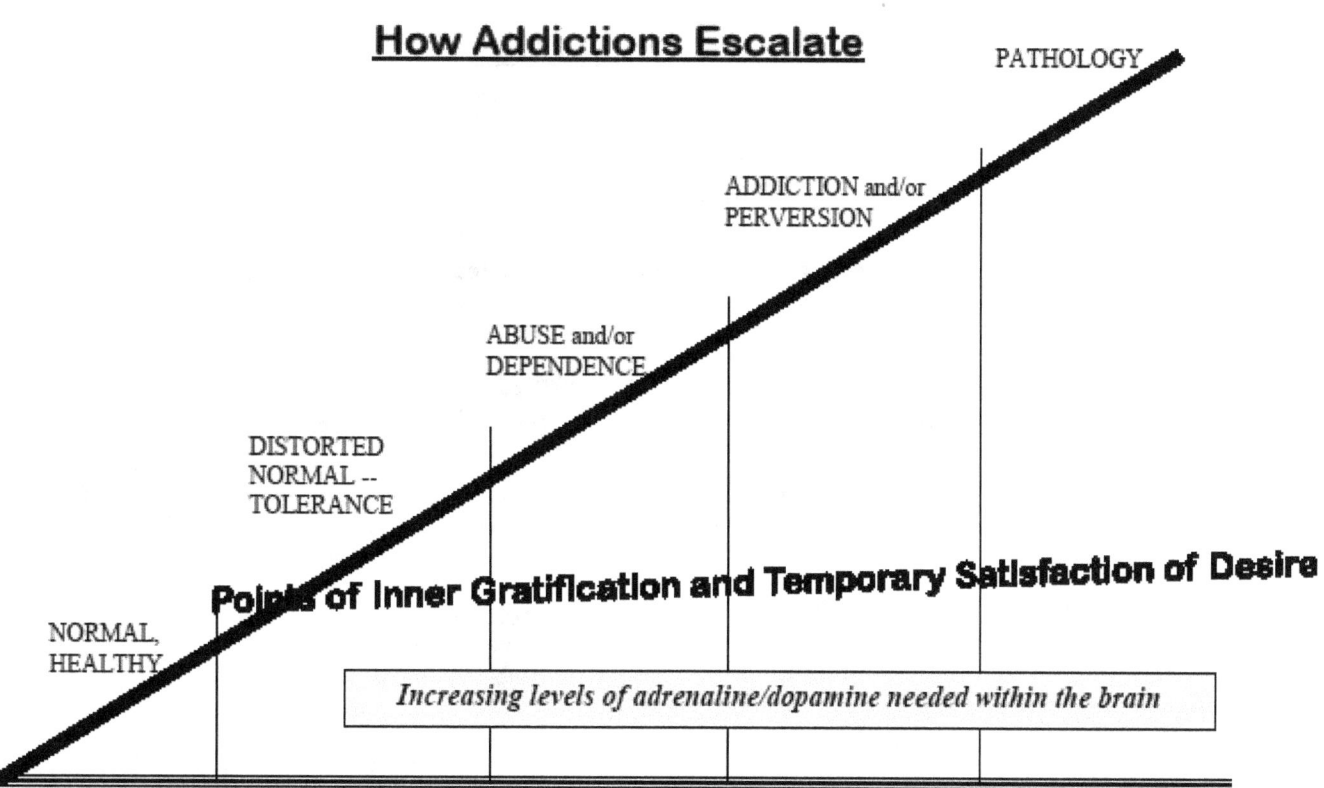

Anger's Path

Life Approach Attitude (model/imprinting)	The Message Believed (about self) (activator/trigger)	First Emotion (below the surface)	Secondary Emotion (evident behavior)
Everyone should just be nice and get along.	People should listen when I tell them how to get along.	Hurt; Fear of Rejection Fear of Conflict	**ANGER**
My life should be easier than it is.	Life should be fair; Others should take care of me.	Exclusion; Justice Frustration; Insecurity	**ANGER**
I need everyone to respect/like me.	There is something wrong with me.	Rejection: Disapproval Shame; Confusion	**ANGER**
I should be in control of what happens in my life.	Other people should allow me to have the control.	Fear of Vulnerability Fear of Rejection	**ANGER**
I should always know what to do when bad things happen in my life.	I don't know what to do in this situation. I am relationally un-tooled.	Embarrassment Fear of Rejection Fear of Being Known	**ANGER**
I should always be "on top" of things	I can't meet the expectations I have/others have.	Shame; Helplessness Self-Hatred	**ANGER**
Mistakes/Failings are unacceptable.	If I fail, or am wrong, I am unacceptable.	Fear of Disapproval Abandonment; Self-Hatred	**ANGER**
I should use my skills, and not do things I feel are beneath me.	Others should do the things I don't want to do for me.	Entitlement Improper Self-Image	**ANGER**
I should never make mistakes.	I cannot be wrong, or apologize/admit weakness.	Pride; Entitlement; Confusion Shame; Fear of Vulnerability	**ANGER**
I have to earn my way.	My value is determined by what I know how to do.	Overwhelmed; Fear of Rejection; Self-rejection; Guilt; Futility	**ANGER**

CONFLICT OCCURS

©2010 dg/atg

The Illusion of Control

1. We are born. Early self-concept tells us that our parents are powerful.

2. We begin to grow, and see life modeled around us. As children, we believe that we are part of our parents; their powers are ours to share. These powers will give us complete control of ourselves and the world around us.

3. Reality confronts us with the end of illusion that we are all powerful – adolescence or early adulthood.

4. Maturity develops. We realize we are less powerful and more vulnerable than we imagined.

Control – clinging to the illusion that we are all powerful, rather than admitting, accepting and embracing the reality of our own vulnerability.

Control becomes a self-imposed self-image.

It is a form of denial.

We are acting in codependency when we enable the bad behavior of others.

Enabling means removing the natural consequences of a person's bad behavior.

Healthy Control	**Unhealthy Control**
I have a sense of personal effectiveness, and am aware I am able to effect change within my sphere of influence.	*I assume I have more power than I actually do, and seek to force change based upon my own beliefs & emotion.*
I realize I only have control over those areas of living directly related to me.	*I try to coerce, threaten, cajole, and manipulate others in order to see my desires come to fruition.*
I know I have individual significance and value.	*I try to prove my individual significance and value.*
Vulnerability means I have the opportunity to learn and experience true community, while continuing to grow and learn.	*Vulnerability means I am at risk to experience shame, ridicule, criticism, a discovery of mistakes, rejection and/or failure.*
When I am anxious, I reach for relationship as a sort of life-ring, helping me not to sink into depression.	*When I am anxious, I reach for relationship because I want a life-guard (person) to rescue me from what I feel.*
I am content and living my life. I tell myself, "I am enjoying ____."	*I am racing, and have no time. I tell myself, "Life will begin when ____."*
I sometimes have to fight for how I would like to spend my day.	*I sometimes feel I need to tell others how they should spend their day.*
My relationships are more important to me my need to be right or to win.	*My relationships are dependent upon whether I am seen as right and/or winning.*

Levels of Communication

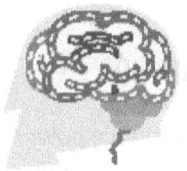

1. Clichés

2. Facts

Task & Doing

IQ

Outer Life

IMAGE BASED

Tangible

Wall of self protection—pride+fear=control

Inner Life

Intangible

3. Principles/Values/Morals/Feelings
4. Yearnings/Needs

Relationship & Being

EQ

TRUTH BASED

Line of selfless choice

OBEDIENCE BASED

5. Deep sense of security & approval

IQ & EQ

Core Person (Inner Child)

© dg atg

A Child's Core Needs

These core yearnings/needs must be met during cognitive (physical) development, for a person to have a healthy life-view, and a complete sense of Personhood.

1. A safe secure environment (both physically and emotionally).

2. A constant reinforcement of personal value/worth.

3. Repeated messages that the person is valued, unique, & special

4. Unconditional Love & acceptance

5. Basic Care & nurturing

6. Encouragement to Grow – develop personal gifts & talents.

7. A pathway to fellowship with God

8. Connection & belonging

9. Feeling needed & Useful

10. Inner emotional & character building for destiny fulfillment

"When you give another person the power to define you,
then you also give them the power to control you."
— Leslie Vernick

The Spiritual Significance of An Apology

"And I will give them one heart, and put a new spirit within them. And I will take the heart of stone out of their flesh and give them a heart of flesh, that they may walk in My statutes and keep My ordinances and do them. Then they will be My people, and I shall be their God." Ezek. 11:18-20

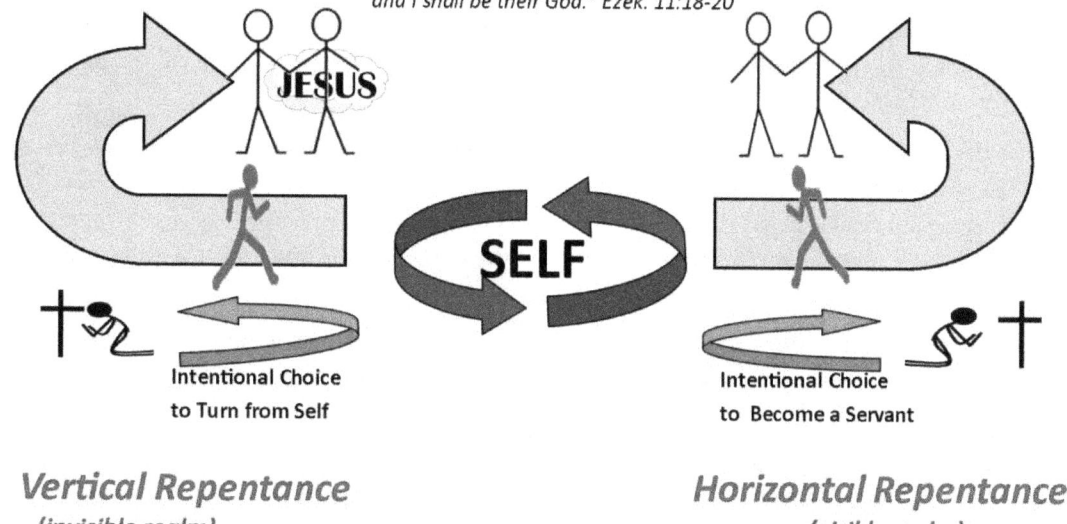

Vertical Repentance
(invisible realm)

Horizontal Repentance
(visible realm)

Four Statements in the Healthy Apology
Healthy Apologies are essential in building Relationships

Note: A true apology is offered whether the other person is ready to reciprocate or not. Also, a true apology does not hold elements of, "I will if you will." When we repent to another person, we do so for the sake of the relationship, because we feel before God it is the right thing to do.

1. "I'm sorry."
We take ownership of our regret, and express our regret over our actions/words to the person who has experienced damaged relationship with us.

2. "I was wrong."
We acknowledge our lack of perfection, and communicate that we made a mistake in the relationship. To take this to its healthiest/deepest level, the "I was wrong statement" should also include the relational territory violated. For example: "I was wrong to speak to you that way," or "I was wrong to embarrass you in front of your friends."

3. "Would you please forgive me?"
We express our desire to continue the relationship, by requesting forgiveness. When we do, we realize that the other person is not immediately required to release us from the offense. In cases of deeper wounding, the ability to forgive might take time for the person to discover. If we try to apologize without forgiveness taking place, we short-circuit the relationship and make it totally one-sided; we avoid the real work of relating well – avoiding inevitable conflict. When we ask for forgiveness, it is a good practice to add the Instance to the end of the question as well. Such as "Would you please forgive me for sending you that signal? I would never want to hurt you that way again, even unintentionally."

4. "What can I do to make things right between us?"
This statement sets a foundation for the healing work of restitution to take place. When we take ownership of our mistakes in relationship, seeking reconciliation and restoration, usually it will require a short period of re-building trust with the person we have injured. This process takes time, and effort.

Vertical Repentance — *(invisible realm, eternal, spiritual)*

1. **When we repent, we are apologizing to God.** *An apology involves more than feeling sorry or regretful over our behavior, or fearful of experiencing the consequences we have earned. The Biblical word translated "repent" from the original language is "metanoeo," which means "to change the way we think, and to amend behaviors." In modern terms, it means "to turn around," or "make a U-turn." (Luke 15:10 and 17:10)*

2. **Repentance involves taking responsibility for our behaviors.** *When we take ownership of our actions, it involves recognizing those areas where we have stepped away from the embrace and relationship of God. Part of this process is the understanding of our own weaknesses in being tempted. James wrote that we are tempted when we are "drawn away." The Greek word for this concept is "exelko," meaning that we are lured away, and break the embrace of relationship. (James 1:4)*

3. **When we repent to God, we are told to admit to Him what we have done wrong. When we do, it opens the door for God's forgiveness in our lives, and begins the process of cleansing and healing our hearts.** *(I John 1:9)*

4. **Maintaining a repentant heart, and seeking to keep our hearts open and soft, keeps us in a healthy place of being in right relationship with God.** *(righteousness= right relationship with God.)*

Horizontal Repentance — *(visible realm, eternal, spiritual)*

1. **When we apologize to another person, we are repenting for sinning against them.** *An apology given to another person is not just saying, "I'm sorry." In a shadow of the power of an apology to God, an apology given to another person, also involves more than feeling sorry or regretful over our behavior, or fearful of experiencing the consequences we have earned. (Ephesians 4:22-32)*

2. **It takes humility to apologize.** *A true apology is more concerned with the damage our actions and/or words have caused in the other person, than we are with clarifying or blaming someone/something for our behaviors. It is more concerned with seeking to understand, than it is with seeking to be understood. When we allow our hearts to become hardened towards another person, we succumb to the deception of Pride, protecting our own rights and sense of entitlement. (James 4:6-10)*

3. **Positional authority is temporary. Relational equity is eternal.** *Our relationships and personal life-lessons, are the only entities we can take with us into the eternal realm. When we defend our image, our position, our rights, or our opinions we develop hardness of heart that separates us from relationship — first with others, then with God. (Romans 12:3-10, I John 4:7-11, Matthew 5:21-25)*

4. **We are called to treat each other the way we would treat Christ Jesus.** *(Matthew 25:31-46)*

5. **An apology opens the door to the process of forgiveness, cleansing, restoration of relationship with another person, and emotional healing. There can be no depth of relationship without the willingness to admit mistakes, misunderstandings and/or failures. We are called to see ourselves as servants of others, rather than seeking to have our rights satisfied.** *(Galatians 5:13-14, Luke 22:24-27, Philippians 2:3-15)*

6. **An apology is only the beginning place for communication and healing to take place.**

Section Four
Assessment and Discovery Tools

Self Assessment – What Elements of Co-Dependency are evidencing themselves in my own life?

To what level do you agree with the following statements:

1. Do you tolerate mistreatment from other people in hopes of being loved?

    _____ Yes   ____No

    If you answered yes, please rate the intensity and frequency of those headaches

    0   1   2   3   4   5   6   7   8   9   10

    ~~~

2. Do you depend on people who are emotionally unavailable to care for you?

    _____ Yes   ____No

    If you answered yes, please rate the intensity and frequency

    0   1   2   3   4   5   6   7   8   9   10

    ~~~~~

3. Are you currently in a relationship with someone who hits you, punches you, or abuses you sexually, emotionally, or verbally?

    _____ Yes   ____No

    If you answered yes, please rate the intensity and frequency

    0   1   2   3   4   5   6   7   8   9   10

4. Do you feel compelled to help people to feel better or to solve their problems?

_____ Yes   _____ No

If you answered yes, please rate the intensity and frequency

0   1   2   3   4   5   6   7   8   9   10

~~~~

5. Do you feel empty, bored or unimportant if you're not helping someone, or responding to a crisis?

_____ Yes   _____ No

If you answered yes, please rate the intensity and frequency

0   1   2   3   4   5   6   7   8   9   10

~~~~

6. Do you rescue others from the consequences of their irresponsible behavior? *(For example, a child who has gotten into financial trouble needs money, and you rescue them in order to shield them.)*

_____ Yes   _____ No

If you answered yes, please rate the intensity and frequency

0   1   2   3   4   5   6   7   8   9   10

~~~~

7. Is it hard for you to say "no" when someone asks you for help?

    _____ Yes   ____No

    If you answered yes, please rate the intensity and frequency

    0   1   2   3   4   5   6   7   8   9   10

8. Is it hard for you to ask for help?

    _____ Yes   ____No

    If you answered yes, please rate the intensity and frequency

    0   1   2   3   4   5   6   7   8   9   10

9. In close relationships do you lose interest in your own life, to show interest and involvement in the other person's life?

    _____ Yes   ____No

    If you answered yes, please rate the intensity and frequency

    0   1   2   3   4   5   6   7   8   9   10

10. Are you quick to become angry about other people and their problems?

    _____ Yes   ____No

    If you answered yes, please rate the intensity and frequency

    0   1   2   3   4   5   6   7   8   9   10

11. Do you often talk about other people and their problems?

_____ Yes   ____No

If you answered yes, please rate the intensity and frequency

0   1   2   3   4   5   6   7   8   9   10

~~~~~

12. Do you worry about other people's opinions of you?

_____ Yes   ____No

If you answered yes, please rate the intensity and frequency

0   1   2   3   4   5   6   7   8   9   10

~~~~~

13. Do you worry about how other people are feeling?

_____ Yes   ____No

If you answered yes, please rate the intensity and frequency

0   1   2   3   4   5   6   7   8   9   10

~~~~~

14. Do you keep quiet to avoid conflicts with people?

_____ Yes   ____No

If you answered yes, please rate the intensity and frequency

0   1   2   3   4   5   6   7   8   9   10

15. Do you feel more comfortable giving to others rather than receiving from others?

_____ Yes _____ No

If you answered yes, please rate the intensity and frequency

0   1   2   3   4   5   6   7   8   9   10

~~~~~

16. Is it hard for you to talk with a boss or someone in authority?

_____ Yes _____ No

If you answered yes, please rate the intensity and frequency

0   1   2   3   4   5   6   7   8   9   10

~~~~~

17. Is it difficult for you to receive attention, compliments, or gifts from others?

_____ Yes _____ No

If you answered yes, please rate the intensity and frequency

0   1   2   3   4   5   6   7   8   9   10

~~~~~

18. I tend to stay in relationships that don't work, and tolerate abuse in order to keep people loving me.

_____ Yes _____ No

If you answered yes, please rate the intensity and frequency

0   1   2   3   4   5   6   7   8   9   10

19. I tend to leave bad relationships, only to form new ones that don't work either.

_____ Yes   ____No

If you answered yes, please rate the intensity and frequency

0   1   2   3   4   5   6   7   8   9   10

~~~~~

20. If someone important to me expects me to do something, I should do it.

_____ Yes   ____No

If you answered yes, please rate the intensity and frequency

0   1   2   3   4   5   6   7   8   9   10

~~~~~

21. It is unacceptable for me to irritable or unpleasant, at times. It makes me unacceptable.

_____ Yes   ____No

If you answered yes, please rate the intensity and frequency

0   1   2   3   4   5   6   7   8   9   10

~~~~~

22. I shouldn't do anything to make others angry at me.

_____ Yes   ____No

If you answered yes, please rate the intensity and frequency

0   1   2   3   4   5   6   7   8   9   10

23. It's usually my fault when someone I love is upset with me.

_____ Yes   _____ No

If you answered yes, please rate the intensity and frequency

0   1   2   3   4   5   6   7   8   9   10

~~~~~

24. Fear of someone else's anger has a lot of influence over what I say and do.

_____ Yes   _____ No

If you answered yes, please rate the intensity and frequency

0   1   2   3   4   5   6   7   8   9   10

~~~~~

25. I should keep the people I love happy.

_____ Yes   _____ No

If you answered yes, please rate the intensity and frequency

0   1   2   3   4   5   6   7   8   9   10

~~~~~

26. I obtain my sense of personal value esteem out of helping others solve their problems. My focus in helping them is how well I did, based on their happiness.

_____ Yes   _____ No

If you answered yes, please rate the intensity and frequency

0   1   2   3   4   5   6   7   8   9   10

27. I tend to overextend myself in taking care of others.

_____ Yes   _____ No

If you answered yes, please rate the intensity and frequency

0   1   2   3   4   5   6   7   8   9   10

~~~~

Self Assessment – How does Co-Dependency Evidence itself in my life?

It is important that in taking this self-assessment, that we realize that everyone has some tendencies to co-dependency. However, when those tendencies stop the development of identity, and conflict with the ability of a person to relate to others in community, in a realistic and honest manner, then those tendencies have formed un-health in the life.

The goal of this assessment is to help you to determine the places in your heart where you have stopped developing in your emotional and spiritual life. What areas of Personhood have stopped growing? These need to be repented of, and life patterns need to be brought into change.

1. Look back over your answers. How many questions did you answer "yes?"

   _____

2. Please count up the number of questions you answered "yes," and circled a number lower than 4.

   _____

3. How many questions did you answer "yes," and circle a number higher than 3?

   _____

(If you answered "yes" to five or more questions, and assessed a value of higher than 3 to each of those, it indicates a strong tendency toward Co-Dependency in your life, and you should seek help in re-evaluating your lifestyle.)

4. Cumulative Scoring: Please add the numbers of the numbers you circled, and assess your risk for depression with the chart below…

30-80 points	**Reasonably Healthy**. Everyone on the planet has some tendency toward Co-Dependency. At the present level, these tendencies in your life are not threatening your ability to determine boundaries in your relationships with those closest to you.
80-150 points	**Losing Touch.** At these levels, your relationships with other people tend to determine your inner sense of acceptance and security. It would help you to seek help from a professional to assess your life approach and priorities. If you don't do something to change your lifestyle soon, you will probably find yourself in a situation of emotional breakdown.
150-270 points	**Danger Zone.** At these levels, a person's life has been become clouded over, with pieces of the identity having been traded away for peace at any cost. Usually, the person has begun to live life without thinking about their own inner hopes or dreams for destiny fulfillment. This person has become a survivor, and many times is afraid to talk about their inner conflicts. It is absolutely essential that you make immediate changes in your lifestyle, and approach to relationships. You should pursue making systematic changes in your life in regard to priorities and daily lifestyle. Seek professional help for objectivity, with help from someone you trust to give you counsel. This is important for spiritual, emotional and physical health.

"How Passive Have I Become in Codependency?"

1. You are giving a friend a ride to church. You get to his house on time, even a little early. He invites you in, and then he putters around the house for another ½ hour, and you realize he is going to make you late. In this situation what do you do?

    a) you get mad, but won't let him know how you feel
    b) you go out to the car and wait, silently fuming
    c) you leave without him, and tell him you need to be on time
    d) you smile outwardly, but inwardly decide to change the
          status of the relationship

2. You are in a hurry to pick a few items from Wal-Mart before guests arrive at your home. You are in the express line, when you realize that the person in front of you has just done their monthly shopping, and the cart is nearly full. What do you do?

    a) you tell the guy behind you that the person in front of you is in the wrong line – loud enough for the person in front of you to hear.
    b) you say nothing, and get inwardly angry and frustrated
    c) you draw the person's attention to the sign stating that they should only have 8 items or less to be in the line you are in
    d) you smile, but inwardly decide to never come to this Wal-Mart again

3. You order a steak to be cooked "rare" at a fancy restaurant, and after a forty-five minute wait, it comes to your table cooked "medium well." What do you do?

    a) you ask to speak to the manager, and angrily inform him that the food critic for the local paper is your best friend.
    b) you eat the steak, and figure you must have ordered the wrong item from the menu
    c) you send it back; asking that your steak be cooked as you ordered it; letting the manager know kindly that someone in the kitchen has messed up, requesting an adjustment on your bill.
    d) You don't want to make waves. You just eat it.

4. You are looking forward to a quiet evening at home, vegetating in front of the television, or with a good book, with no one else around. You really need the quiet, and are looking forward to being alone for the evening. Some friends call and tell you they are on their way over to your house. What do you do?

   a) you suffer through the visit, and then later tell someone who wasn't there how you really felt; knowing it will get back to them.
   b) you don't tell them your plans, and you resign yourself to cleaning up your house, and getting ready for their arrival.
   c) you gently tell them that another time would be better, and that you have already made plans for the evening, and hope they understand.
   d) you just give up on getting down time for the evening.

Please refer to the next page for scoring key.

If you answered A to most of the questions

You tend to be a person who takes personally the actions of others, and many times assumes that they are disregarding you on purpose. You enjoy being the center of any relationship, and are uncomfortable when you are not being catered to. You tend to move in a manipulative manner when you are upset, so that your desires will be recognized. You might be passive aggressive, meaning you become angry as a result of conflict, and have learned to hold on to offenses, blaming others for your own choices to remain passive.

Make a decision to tell yourself "no," when it comes to expecting others to make your life work. Stop demanding that others make your life normal. Repent for keeping record of wrongs, and holding offenses against others. Forgive. Admit your own responsibility, without finding something to blame the difficulty upon, and give the Holy Spirit permission to lead you to a new place of growth.

If you answered B to most of the questions

You tend to be a person who sees yourself as living on the bottom of the food chain. You don't voice your needs, or desires, and find it difficult to express your inner heart to others, even if they express a desire to become closer to you. At some point in your life, you have made a decision that your own desires and feelings were not as important as other people, whether due to disappointment, rejection, or another inner wound in your soul. You are constantly living to make others happy. You most probably are a classic case of a passive person.

Make a decision to believe what the Word of God says about you, and your value to Father God, and to the Body of Christ. Repent for giving in to the victim mentality, and for seeking man's approval instead of God's approval. Choose to strengthen your will, taking action to grow.

If you answered C to most of the questions

You are probably healthier than you realize. You have learned to confront without creating conflict, and you don't take the difficulties of other people around you on to yourself, expecting to be able to have the answers for their problems. You don't mind helping others, but the approval you gain from that service has not become your identity.

Make a decision to serve others, by not being their emotional "guru." You can be a friend, without becoming a source. Ask the Holy Spirit to show you how to minister and serve those around you in areas of care and healing.

If you answered D to most of the questions

You are not only passive, but you are fear motivated. Passivity has begun to ruin even what could be the most positive moments of your life and relationships. You have learned to retreat, and to hide when conflict happens around you. You have stopped making decisions, or resolving conflict. Your method of dealing with conflict is to avoid it.

Make a decision to stop running. Repent for allowing fear and passivity to stop you from growing into the person Father God has destined you to become. Open your heart to the love of Father God, and let Him set you free from the misconceptions about your own personhood, and identity. Ask the Holy Spirit to strengthen your will to believe and receive His unconditional love for you, in every area of your life.

Things Passive People Say

"We should always be logical and consistent, without error."

"Whatever"

"It's okay, I don't mind"

"It's up to you"

"I don't care, what do you want to do?"

"It doesn't matter"

"Don't rock the boat"

"I guess I don't care"

"My feelings aren't important"

"No big deal"

"If I don't make a fuss, and just keep quiet, things will change."

"I don't want to be a bother."

"I don't want to appear needy."

"I don't want to ask for too much."

"I don't want to be a burden."

"I don't want to make waves."

"I don't do things, they happen to me."

"I don't have control of the events and feelings that surround me."

"I will lose relationships if I step out and create boundaries in my life."

"It's shameful to make mistakes."

The Relational Pattern of the Addict/Codependent Relationship

Controlled Maintenance

Addict/Narcissist in center of relational orbit. Codependent coping/pleasing and controlling.

Codependent's pattern continues. Resentment, misunderstanding, and anger builds to exhaustion.

CONFLICT (not resolved)

A sense of fragile harmony continues, with each avoiding conflict. Roles reverse, with codependent taking center of relational orbit.

Silence; Maintenance

A sense of fragile harmony continues, with each avoiding conflict. Roles reverse, with codependent taking center of relational orbit.

"Don't leave me." Reinforcement of Denial

Am I Addicted?

Addiction comes in many different forms. If you wonder whether any of your day-to-day behaviors might be habitually more out of control than under personal discipline ... Please take time to ask yourself the questions listed in this questionnaire.

Please assign a number to each statement:
1) All the time   2) Some of the time   3) A little   4) Not at all

1 2 3 4	1. Do thoughts of the substance/person/activity interfere with your social life?
1 2 3 4	2. Do thought patterns of the substance/person/activity cause issues in how you relate to your friends?
1 2 3 4	3. Do your thoughts about the substance/person/activity interfere with your family life?
1 2 3 4	4. When you think about the substance/person/activity, is the focus mainly upon personal happiness, before it is about deepening the relationship?
1 2 3 4	5. Do you hide, or lie about your activities relating to the substance/person/activity?
1 2 3 4	6. Do images of the substance/person/activity cause disruptions and distractions while you are working?
1 2 3 4	7. Have you at times lost the ability to concentrate on your job, because you are thinking about the substance/person/activity?
1 2 3 4	8. Have you been accused of being obsessed/distracted by the substance/person/activity?
1 2 3 4	9. Do you find yourself hiding your thoughts about the substance/person/activity when you are with family members or friends?
1 2 3 4	10. Have you found yourself to have an increasing widening appetite in regard to the substance/person/activity related materials and/or activities?
1 2 3 4	11. Do you have difficulty thinking of the substance/person/activity with undistracted thought; you can do without it and not feel deprived?
1 2 3 4	12. When you meet someone new, is it part of the beginning of your conversation to discuss the substance/person/activity?

Please turn the page for Scoring key.

Key:

Count up your "1's" _____

Count up your "2's" _____

Count up your "3's" _____

Count up your "4's" _____

What is your total? _____/48

    The higher the score, the safer your approach and attitude toward giving in to addictive behavior. All addictions begin in the mind.

    Any circled 1 is an indication of present addiction issues.
    Any circled 2 is an indication of a difficulty with presently being drawn toward addiction.
    Any circled 3 is an indication of an inclination or tendency/temptation towards addiction.

Both "1" and "2" answers also indicate a difficulty in imprinting and/or development issues in regard to healthy trust and relationship in regard to community and vulnerability.

"3" answers indicate a sense of confusion in regard to areas of development in healthy emotionality and identity.

"4" answers indicate areas of healthy emotionality and identity formation.

Am I Sexually Addicted?

Sexual addiction comes in many different forms. If you find yourself habitually involved in <u>any</u> of the <u>behaviors</u> listed below – please take time to ask yourself the questions listed in this questionnaire.

<u>Sexual Behaviors</u>: *Sexual Fantasy, Internet Pornography, Masturbation, Pornography (film, video, magazine), Illicit books, Strip clubs, Prostitution, Exhibitionism, Exploitation (sexual use) of others, illicit chat rooms/sites/games*

Please assign a number to each statement:
1) All the time   2) Some of the time   3) A little   4) Not at all

1 2 3 4	1. Do thoughts of sex interfere with your social life?
1 2 3 4	2. Do thought patterns of sex, or sexual images cause issues in how you relate to your friends?
1 2 3 4	3. Do your thoughts about sex interfere with your family life?
1 2 3 4	4. When you think about the sex act, is the focus mainly upon personal release, before it is about deepening the relationship?
1 2 3 4	5. Do you hide, or lie about your activities relating to sex? (pornography, fetishes, prostitution, etc.)
1 2 3 4	6. Do images of sex cause disruptions and distractions while you are working?
1 2 3 4	7. Have you at times lost the ability to concentrate on your job, because you are thinking about sex?
1 2 3 4	8. Have you been accused of sexual harassment?
1 2 3 4	9. Do you find yourself hiding your thoughts about sex when you are with family members or friends?
1 2 3 4	10. Have you found yourself to have an increasing widening appetite in regard to sex and sexually related materials?
1 2 3 4	11. Do you have difficulty thinking of sex as a tender expression of love within a committed marriage relationship?
1 2 3 4	12. When you meet someone of the opposite sex, do you undress them in your mind?

Please turn the page
For scoring key

Key:

Count up your "1's" _____

Count up your "2's" _____

Count up your "3's" _____

Count up your "4's" _____

What is your total? _____/48

The higher the score, the safer your approach and attitude toward sexual behavior. All addictions begin in the mind.

Any circled 1 is an indication of sexual addiction issues.
Any circled 2 is an indication of a difficulty with sexual addiction.
Any circled 3 is an indication of a tendency/temptation towards sexual addiction.

Both "1" and "2" answers also indicate a difficulty in imprinting and/or development issues in regard to healthy trust and relationship with the opposite sex.

"3" answers indicate a sense of confusion in regard to areas of development in healthy sexuality and identity.

"4" answers indicate areas of healthy sexuality and identity formation.

How Important to Me Are the Opinions of Other People?

Please assign a value to each of the statements below. Use the following scale:
0= never true   1= rarely true   2= frequently true   3= usually true

_____ 1. I must be perfect in my attitudes and appearance or I will be rejected.

_____ 2. If I make a mistake, something horrible will happen.

_____ 3. When I do things perfectly, I will be accepted.

_____ 4. If I don't do things "right" I will be embarrassed.

_____ 5. When I get it right, I will finally accept myself.

_____ 6. If others do not approve of me, then I am not okay.

_____ 7. If authority figures accept and approve of me, then I am spiritually okay.

_____ 8. I don't think I will ever be good enough.

_____ 9. Things should be done the right way.

_____ 10. If I do things well, I will be noticed, and accepted.

_____ 11. When things go wrong, I need to fix them so everyone will be happy.

_____ 12. It falls to me to keep the peace in my home.

_____ 13. I must keep a clean environment. Order brings approval.

_____ 14. When I make mistakes, I feel worthless.

_____ 15. I cannot allow myself to fail.

_____ 16. God accepts me when I have covered all of my bases.

_____ **TOTAL**

KEY
0-16--------------- *Normal amount of relational adjustments. The lower the score, the healthier your thinking patterns.*
17-32---------------*Definite pattern of adjusting caregiving based upon acceptance and approval from others.*
33-48---------------*Unhealthy fear and codependent issues definitely present.*

> *"There are two questions a man must ask himself:*
> *The first is 'Where am I going?'*
> *and the second is 'Who will go with me?'*
> *If you ever get these questions in the wrong order you are in trouble."*
>
> Sam Keen

Section Five
The Counselor's Role in the Healing Journey

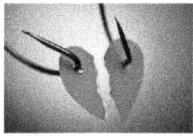

Helping a client understand the structure of the Addiction/Codependent System, can also become a tool in helping them to decipher and dismantle their Issues.

Whenever an addiction is present, the true addiction is not the substance, but the chemical release of dopamine in the brain, that brings a euphoric sense of peace and tranquility. The pain goes away for a little while, and an addict becomes deceived into believing first that they can manage their need, and then they begin to realize they need more and more of the substance in question just to feel good again. ("Monkey on my Back" illustration). The Monkey becoming a Gorilla the addict can no longer carry is how the disease progresses – in the end it destroys a person's ability to function without it.

Why Does An Abused Woman Believe She Should Stay?
From Olympia Union Gospel Mission

Her abuser will not allow her to leave: Abusers may go to extremes to prevent their victims from leaving. They may provide victims many reassurances and demonstrations of the consequences of leaving.

Fear for her survival: She is fearful that the abuser will find her and kill or harm her, her children, or her relatives, or otherwise retaliate. He may have made such threats and may have weapons. Seventy-five percent of domestic violence homicides and calls for police help take place *after* the victim leaves.

Fear of being alone/lonely: Many abusers strive to isolate their victims from social contact or support in order to make them more dependent, and often try to convince them that they are socially unacceptable and worthless. As a result, the victim may fear unbearable loneliness.

Fear of being on her own: She doesn't think she can cope with being a single parent, adjust to life alone, and perhaps face a bewildering array housing, employment, childcare, legal system, and transportation challenges. This fear may be heightened by physical or mental/emotional injury she has suffered from the abuse, or if she has a disability. Her abuser may have caused her question her own sanity, especially if he has been telling her and others she is crazy. She may not think she will find someone else.

Lack of resources: She may not have economic independence to support herself and her children. Many abusers will sequester control over all family assets, and court settlements can take years. She may not have been able to find adequate resources in the community for housing, rental deposits, transportation, childcare, employment, legal representation, or medical assistance for herself and her children. If she leaves, files charges, or seeks help, her partner may lose his job or his career, eliminating the possibility of receiving child support.

Coercion: He may have threatened to take the children, to "out" her publicly, to spread lies about her, or to call immigration if she leaves. He may have threatened to kill or harm her relatives.

Concern for her partner: Her abuser may have threatened suicide if she leaves. She may feel sorry or responsible for him, or concerned that he will lose his job, office, or social standing. She may still love her partner, who may not be violent all the time. She may believe that she can save him if she stays.

Lack of Support: Her abuser may be a respected and popular member of the community, and she may fear that no one will believe her. The abuser may have worked to convince others that she is to blame, or is crazy. Her family may be afraid to take her in, may blame her for the abuse, or may tell her it is her responsibility to stay in the relationship. She may have no one to talk to about her problem.

Concern for her children: She does not want to deprive her children of a father. She may be concerned about the possible effects of disrupting their lives and of divorce.

Responsibility: She may feel like, or have been told, that it is up to her to work things out and save the relationship. Her abuser may have convinced her that she caused the abuse and the relationship problems.

Shame, embarrassment, and humiliation: "Know one must know." She may feel that the abuse is a bad reflection on her and her family, or that leaving the relationship is a sign of failure on her part.

Faith: She may believe that the tenets of her faith require her to remain in the relationship in spite of the abuse. She may fear rejection by her faith community.

Cultural and social: Family and friends may pressure her to stay. People may blame her for the causing the abuse. Her culture may disapprove of women who leave their marriage and "break up the family". She may face language or cultural barriers if she seeks help from the larger community.

Denial: "It's not really so bad." "He didn't break any bones." "The children don't know."

Hope or optimism: She may hope against hope that things will get better. She may think that the abuse will end because her abuser has started counseling or a perpetrator treatment program. Her abuser may become remorseful after battering, and promise not to do it again; he may be a model partner for a while.

Gender roles: A male abuser may convince a female victim that the man is the head of the house and has the right to set and enforce rules, and women and children must obey and meet the needs of the head of the household. She may believe that women should be submissive, passive, nurturing, and put their own needs last.

Chemical dependency: If she abuses alcohol or drugs as a means of coping with the abuse, she may be less clear and strong, making it difficult to leave.

Normalization: She may have been a victim of child abuse or witnessed her father abusing her mother, and believes abuse is normal.

Previous failed attempts: She may have tried to leave before but failed. She may be a victim of mishandling by agencies and is afraid to seek help again. She may have failed to receive help or protection from law enforcement or social service agencies.

Fear of losing employment: The victim may fear losing her job because of missed work, disruption, or the need to go into hiding. (75% of abusers will harass their victims at work, by phone or in person). Who will stay home to care for a sick child?

"There is a difference between perseverance and control. One flows from a strong will, the other from a strong "won't."

Henry Ward Beecher

"Whatever you are not willing to confront, even in yourself, you are willing to live with."

A person's stage of maturity is definitely a factor when it comes to dealing with Addiction/Codependency issues. (For a more complete addressing of this issue, please refer to the handbooks in our series entitled, "A Christian Counselor's Primer on Emotional Development." Emotional Development is always a factor in a person's Addiction/Codependency issues. The process of development requires coaching, teaching, counseling and support as a client walks through the recovery/re-programming journey.

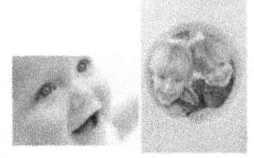

From Child to Adult
Steps to Emotional Maturity

Childhood	Developing Lesson	Adulthood
NO MOTIVATION	Learns to do everything in life for the sake of doing the right thing at the right time — which is Virtue	SENSE OF PURPOSE
REQUIRES INSTRUCTION In order to survive	Discovers that everyone is insecure, and has areas where Life is unknown. Choosing to ask for and seek out help and instruction. This is teachability.	ASKS FOR INSTRUCTION In order to grow
External motivation	Takes responsibility to follow through to completion even those projects and assignments I find unpleasant. Discovers a sense of personal satisfaction in that effort.	Internal motivation
Fear prevents bad behavior	Discovers the depth to which personal negative behaviors affect those in their circles of relationship. Chooses to maintain those relationships rather than satisfy personal urges.	Love/purpose become reasons For healthy Behavior
Shame wants to keep things hidden; maintain image of goodness to gain approval	Realizes that everything happening in our lives is eventually discovered. Choosing to know and be known within safe relationship. Discovering that false images are destructive.	Brings flaws to light in order to heal; honest with self
Avoids getting into trouble; fear of Punishment/disapproval	In light of Christ's love and grace, is willing to own and confess when a mistake is made. Owns responsibility without blame.	Does the right thing, even at personal cost
Avoids discussing unpleasant subjects	Has discovered that everyone on the planet has areas where they are untooled, or uneducated. Has learned the value of non-defensive teachability. Desires to grow.	"Please help me with this"
Seeks to prevent anger from authority figures	Has learned to be open, and known as circumstances happen. Has discovered personal value in relationship with God, so is no longer threatened. Has chosen to value others above self.	Seeks to guard relationship w/ authority figures; accountable
Philippians 3:19 — Driven by flesh God=appetite/Glory= shame	Maturity cannot be rushed. Discovery cannot be forced. Emotional Development takes us from "what's in this for me?" to "what is the right thing for me to do, & when?"	*I Corinthians 13:11— led by love speak, think & reason as an adult*

© atg/dcg

What is Needed......

There are steps to growth, and levels of maturity. None can be skipped, but each must be learned. Many clients, because of traumatic events, or unaddressed growth points, feel "stuck" in one stage of development or another. The contrasting list below provides an idea of what to address in dealing with a client in differing levels of emotional development.

Stages of Development

1. Newborn babes (milk/carried)

2. Toddlers (fed/demanding)

3. Small child (feeds self; needs care)

4. Adolescent (resists growth; wants persuasion)

5. Young adult (admits need; asks questions)

6. Adult (follows; learns obedience)

7. Reproducing Adult (selfless disciple)

Stages of Surrender

1. Must learn how to hear the call of Jesus

2. Learning to obey; Follow the call, with their "stuff"

3. Must leave independence; receiving love of God

4. Learn to focus; without distraction

5. Choosing to live in alignment; not rebellious

6. Admitting need for community; seeking Jesus (vulnerability)

7. Leaving substitutions behind; not image based

From the View of A Narcissist

This cute little vignette gives an insight into the mind of the concrete thinking, self-centered narcissist.

A little boy was on the front yard playing roughly with his tormented cat. When they got to making a substantial amount of noise, his father heard it, and came to the front door. "Jimmy, are you pulling that cat's tail?" "No, Papa," the little boy answered, his big blue eyes wide with innocence. "I'm just keeping her tail in my hand. She's the one doing the pulling." Most narcissists have difficulty understanding the aftermath of their actions; tending to blame others. After all, they were just......

The next story can be used to help a narcissist gain a larger perspective on the effects of their actions upon the relationships in their sphere of influence.

Jessica likes to run the show. When she goes out with friends, for example, she chooses the day, the time, and the restaurant. If that isn't enough, once the restaurant host selects a table, Lillian almost always requests something different. Her friends have come to call it the "Jessica switch." She even tells her companions what to eat, and she dominates the flow of conversation. If Lillian doesn't get her way, she picks apart the place that her friends select, or spends the evening sulking. A few of Lillian's friends put up with her controlling ways, but many leave the relationship. Surely she knows what her dictatorial behavior does to people. So why does she do it?

Emotional Qualities of Someone who Struggles with Control Issues
(born of Codependency)

1. Do not feel safe unless they are in control of their environment and relationships.

2. Are stressed because they cannot admit that controlling behavior requires more effort than they have energy.

3. Have difficult relaxing because they anticipate being criticized, shamed, humiliated or rejected.

4. Deal with emotions of excessive vulnerability and low personal value.

5. Are compulsive drivers. Hyper-vigilant; hyper-responsible.

6. Are unaware of the realistic effects of their words/actions on others. They mistakenly believe the control is necessary and helpful.

Even when a codependent person encounters someone with healthy boundaries, the codependent person still operates in their own system; they're not likely to get too involved with people who have healthy boundaries. This, of course, creates problems which continue to recycle; if codependent people can't get involved with people who have healthy behaviors and coping skills, then the problems continue into each new relationship.

Are You The Adult Child of an Addict?

1. Adult children of addicts have to guess at what healthy or normal behavior would look like.

2. Adult children of addicts take themselves very seriously.

3. Adult children of addicts have difficulty following through with a project, from beginning to the end.

4. Adult children of addicts judge themselves without mercy.

5. Adult children of addicts sometimes lie when it would be easier to tell the truth.

6. Adult children of addicts have difficulty with emotional intimacy.

7. Adult children of addicts usually feel that they are different from other people.

8. Adult children of addicts tend to over-react to changes over which they have no control.

9. Adult children of addicts are extremely loyal, even when there is evidence that the loyalty is undeserved or even misplaced.

10. Adult children of addicts constantly seek approval and affirmation from others.

11. Adult children of addicts are either very responsible, or run from responsibility.

12. Adult children of addicts tend to be impulsive; they don't consider the outcome of their actions. As a result, they tend to confusion, self-loathing, and loss of control in their environment when things go wrong.

13. Adult children of addicts feel guilty when they have fun, or enjoy themselves.

14. Adult children of addicts would rather over-do, than under-do.

15. Adult children of addicts struggle with a sense of shame (not being good enough), and so tend to be perfectionistic in their patterns of living.

A person's actions are the result of several foundational factors. Everyone on the planet has damaged beliefs in one area of living or another. The key to healthy development is how each of us respond when we discover we are wrong in what we have come to hold onto as truth. Persons who live with Addiction and/or Codependency are in the situation they are in because they have accepted certain lies as truth, and have adapted their living style to suit those perceptions. It is helpful to take apart the following chart with a client, and help them make discoveries as to the "why's" and "what's" of their behavior choices.

Determination Chart

1. Beliefs—
What we believe about how life works as it relates to our own lives, based upon what has shaped us; our experiences, training & modeling.

2. Choices --
Our Perceptions and Evaluations of How Life Works, based on what we have seen work in the past.

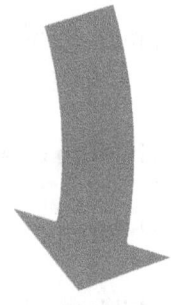

4. Actions –
What we do, moving upon what we assess to be actual and true. These actions reinforce our beliefs, and serve as foundation for greater beliefs.

3. Feelings –
What our inner being tells us is true for in regard to life direction; how we must function for survival.

© atg/dcg

Recovery

1. Recovery from an addiction begins when a person admits they have an addiction, and that they have allowed themselves to substitute their substance or practice for a relationship with God.

2. Recovery begins to empower the person, when true repentance for the substitution happens. This means the person chooses to trust God with all aspect of their life.

3. Recovery is the process of regaining ground that has been given away to the enemy of our souls. It is a painful, tedious, and work-intensive process. It does not happen for passive people. It happens for disciples, who make intentional growth choices.

4. Recovery continues when an addict stops choosing their own feelings and desires, and considers the needs and feelings of others in their sphere of influence.

5. Recovery takes root when an addict learns to put into life practice, the process of telling themselves "NO!" and telling Abba Father "YES!" -- When realization takes place that there can be no compromise with their tendency to addiction, and that there is no middle ground.

6. Recovery takes humility and ongoing acceptance of the Holy Spirit's correction, guidance, comfort, love and direction, through trustworthy leaders and authority figures placed in the life of the addict by Abba Father.

7. Recovery from the tendency to addiction, is the recovery from the fallen human condition, known as "Sin." I am responsible for my own life choices, and I must give account for my own life before God, without blaming others. Therefore, I choose to live in accountability and honesty.

8. Recovery means becoming a safe and trustworthy person, and choosing to move forward in my own growth daily.

What Does the Need to Bond Teach Us When we are Children?

1. The Benefits of Having Relationship
   a. We learn what morality means – right and wrong
   b. We learn how to handle stress – we have a basis of reality for our lives when the stressful period comes to an end
   c. Relationships give meaning to our accomplishments and achievements

2. When we don't learn to bond – we go through three stages of isolation
   a. protest
   b. Depression and despair
   c. Detachment – this is when addiction sets in

3. When we don't know how to open our lives to other people on a core level, we will experience many of the following:

Depression	Despondency
Feelings of purposelessness	Fears of intimacy
Feelings of wretchedness/guilt	Feelings of unreality
Anxiety	Temper and Anger
Inaccurate thinking	Too much caretaking
Hollowness	Fantasy
Addiction	Codependency

However, there are barriers to Bonding

1. We remember past Injuries and fear their repetition

2. We have learned Inaccurate Thinking – we believe the enemy's lies to be true, and our wrong perceptions become reality

3. We hide behind our Defense Mechanisms – Denial, Blame, Believing we have no value, Living on the Defensive, Becoming Preoccupied/Busy, Substitutions, Addictions

These patterns can be ingrained in our family lives, passed down from one generation to another, and then molded into the personal habit patterns in which we live.

Many times, I find it is helpful to ask a client to create a family tree, in order to help the person make discoveries as to the tendencies and compulsions shared and passed down in their lineage. We also use it to determine patterns of relationship, helping the client connect what has been modeled with their own forms of relating to others.

What has been modeled for you – what lives in your family tree?

Family Diagrams

Fill in the boxes in the family tree below with name of corresponding family members. If you need to create a second tree to accommodate a step/blended family, please do so. This will help you understand the influence your family has had upon your choices and emotional development.

After filling in the names, mark each person with a symbol. Did they have an addiction? Were they compulsive? Did they have strong relationships with others, or fragmented relationships? Was there abuse present in the relationship?

☐ Male ◯ Female ╲ Strong & Healthy Connection/Relationship ∿ Strife Filled Relationship/ Separation

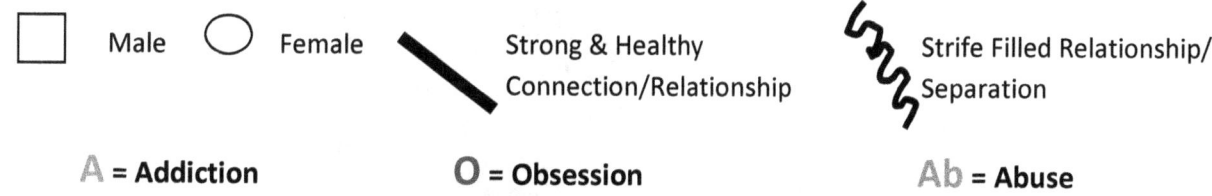

A = **Addiction** O = **Obsession** Ab = **Abuse**

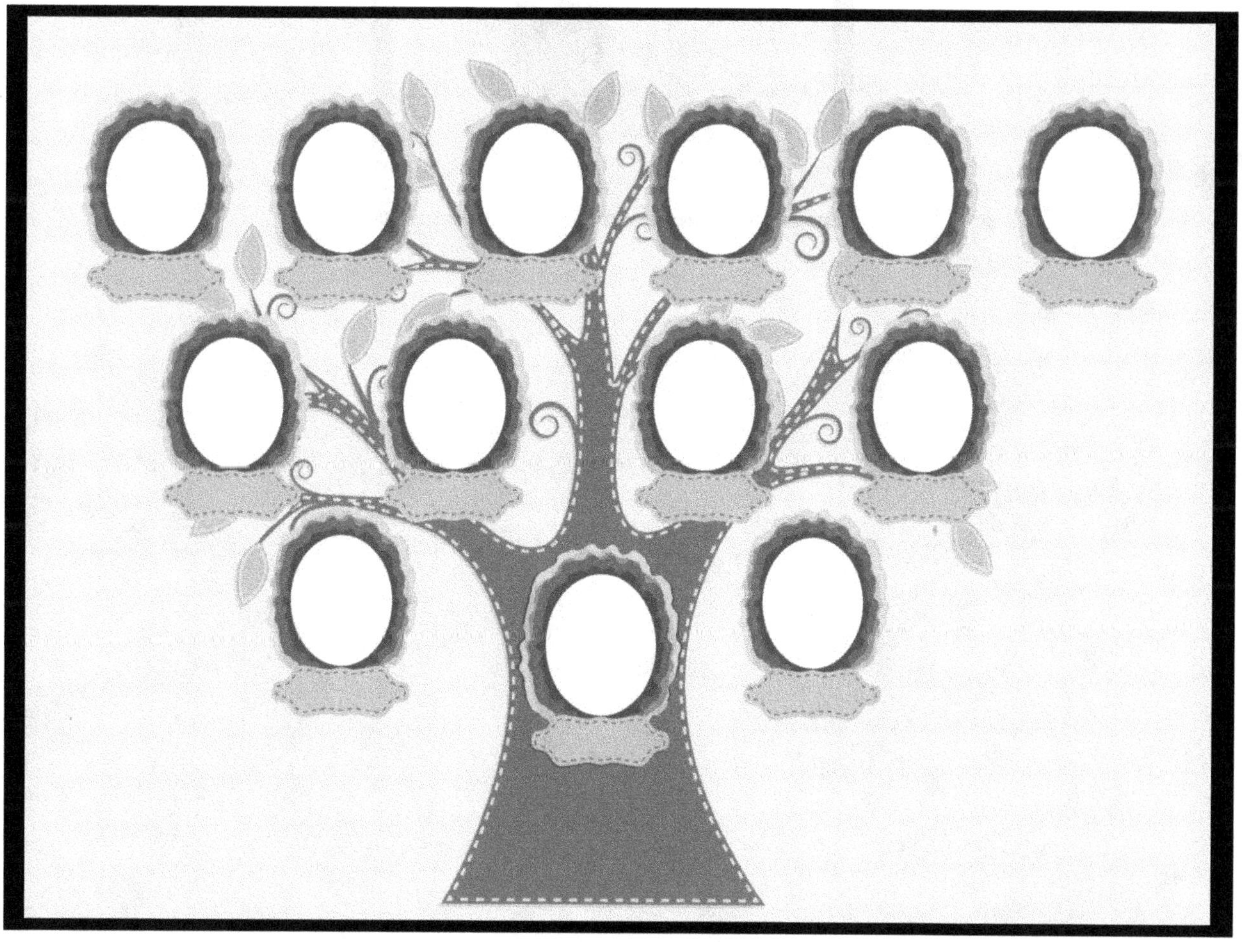

Required Choices to Heal

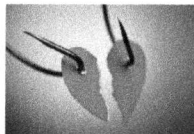

The Contrasting Personal Orbits of Inner Life

1. ## The Soulful Orbit – Sensual

   The soul: **What I think**, based upon **my own** understanding of what is true
       What I feel, based upon **my own** personal perceptions
       What I choose, based upon what provides **me** approval, comfort, or safety

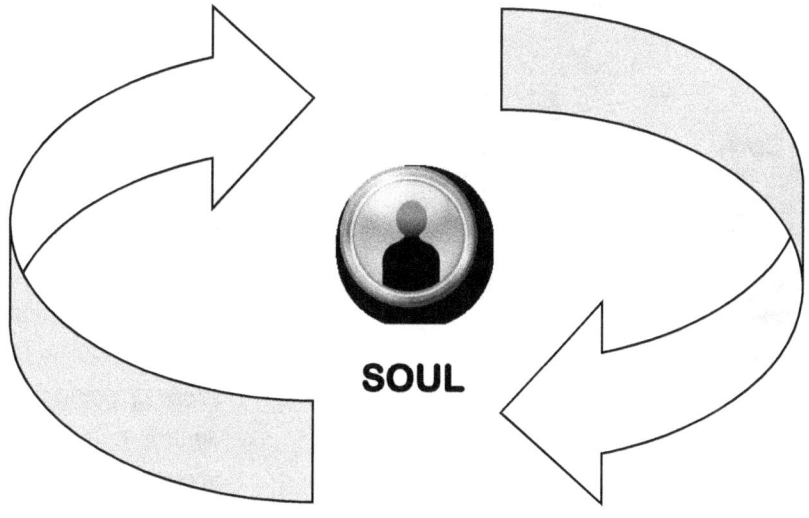

A person with a soulful orbit of life allows personal comfort to drive their life. All relationships entering into the life are expected to also fulfill the person's comfort. All things pursued are for the end result of personal gratification. *"My perceptions determine what is true." "Disagreeing with truth frees me to pursue my own comfort without penalty."*

Before a person is born again, this is the personal orbit of their existence. Life is about survival. Life is about escaping pain of trauma, disappointment and failure. Life is about personal comfort and gratification.

The human spirit is dead in sin, and must become re-born into the spiritual realm, in order for an inner awareness and relationship with the Creator of life to occur. Without this rebirth, we operate in two parts only; soul and body – without the ability to hear the Holy Spirit of God.

We are therefore ruled, or driven, before rebirth, by the need to find that connection and comfort which only the Holy Spirit of God can provide. The elements in the soul which rule us are the emotions, mind, and will; with the emotions and thought patterns feeding into the will, which then makes decisions for daily living.

©atg,dcg

The Submitted Spirit Orbit – Re-Born, Alive

The human spirit: **Communion;** the connection and relationship I have with my Creator, and the acknowledgement that Jesus Christ is God – having all authority and power in my personal life. Choosing to be at one with that essence of His Person and Presence
What I perceive, based upon **directed relationship with Jesus Christ, my Creator, and His truth.**
My intuition, based upon the acceptance and understanding of my personal design, place, and purpose in God's plan. Choosing to **obey that plan, more than my own desires.**

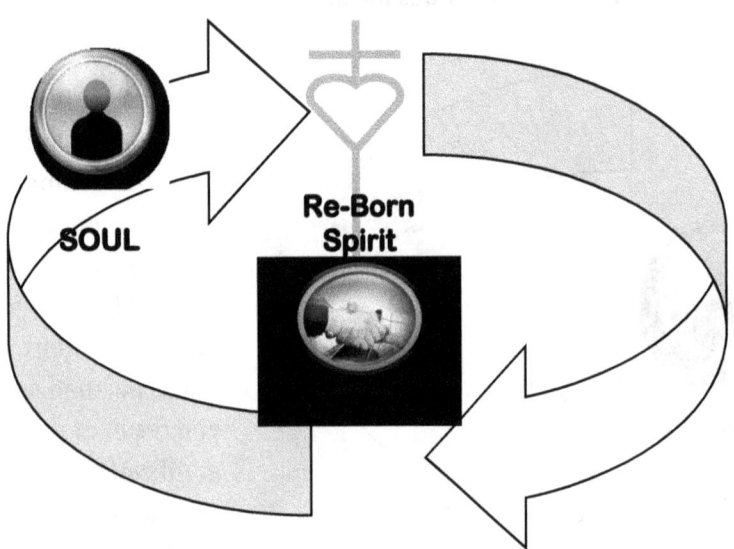

A person with a submitted spirit orbit is led, rather than driven, in life motivation. All relationships entering into the life are seen as provided by Abba Father, to develop personhood and character in the life. All things pursued are for the end result of developing the nature of Jesus within the life. *"The Word of God determines what is True." "I will accept Truth for change." "What I want is no longer the most important thing."*

When a person becomes born again, the personal orbit of their existence becomes about pleasing Abba Father. Life is about growth and development. Life is about healing, rather than escaping, those areas of pain and past trauma within the life.

The human spirit has become alive, resurrected if you will, and begins the process of connecting a person's heart and mind with the Holy Spirit of God, thereby releasing an inner awareness and relationship with the Creator of life to occur. The soulful orbit must be completely done away with, by way of intentional surrender and yielding to the Spirit of God and His plan. In this way, a believer learns to become Holy Spirit led, hearing the voice of God daily. We are body, soul and spirit. The elements in the human spirit connect us with the Spiritual and Eternal realm: the intuition, the perception of truth, and Communion. From this communion flow all elements of connection and understanding with Jesus Christ, and our Abba Father. This is active, rather than passive, and involves all elements of the soul, which now operates in orbit around the Spirit of God. The center of the life is no longer "self," but it now, "Spirit." Rather than being about survival, daily life now centers upon development and growth, seeking to be "salt" and "light" in our spheres of influence in daily living.

©atg, dcg

When a Codependent exercises control they are usually unaware of the effects their words and actions have on those around them.

Control is always about what we do – not who we are.

Steps to Managing Health in Relationships

It is a good idea to choose one of these things.
Work on making one a reality, and then move on to another.
Most overachievers (codependents) try to change everything all at once.
Health just doesn't work that way.

1. Allow yourself to slow down. Make a conscious choice to rest, without activity, for at least a part of each day. Realize that being busy does not mean being important. Picture yourself as a hamster on a wheel – *with a pause button.*

2. Make a choice to hold in your advice and opinions when you are in a group of people, unless those opinions or views are asked for. Listen to the discussions that take place around you. You might be surprised at how much you can learn about the people you are with.

3. Make a decision to allow others in your life to make decisions. If you disagree with their decisions, allow them to discover their own mistakes and grow from what they discover.

4. Begin a discovery journey. Where did you learn to pick up control? Can you remember a decision you made to take up control, or was it modeled for you? Begin to look at those instances in your past, and allow them to come to a place of healing.

5. Repent for taking the place of control in others' lives. In doing so, you have made yourself and your own thought patterns greater and more important than those of other people. Ask the Holy Spirit to teach you how to become a servant, even in your inner life and relationships.

    Scriptures to help: Philippians 2:3-4   I Corinthians 13:4-7
                                          Ephesians 4:28-32   I Thessalonians 5:12-22

6. Begin to reduce your anxiety level. It has been said that anxiety is the interest paid on trouble before the due date. Take time to take care of yourself – a long bath, get a massage, exercise.

7. Grit your teeth and delegate. Allow others to learn. You can coach them as they learn, but make a decision not to critique, amend, correct, improve, upgrade or even stamp your identity on what they have done. You don't have to be in charge.

8. Give up the "if only's" and "I should haves." No one is perfect. Realize that the emotion of regret is simply an indicator of mistakes we can learn from.

9. Defer to others whenever you can. Give them credit for their suggestions, their ideas, and their concepts. Try to refrain from "tooting your own horn," whenever possible.

10. Learn the names of people you see every day, but who do not directly affect your life. Everyone likes to be remembered.

11. Determine that you will not become passive, or pushy. Turn down the volume on your personal life – but don't turn off the music.

12. Know where you can and cannot exert influence. Then, don't force your influence on others. Lead without coercion. Control is the effort to dominate. Leadership is the silent effort of influence.

13. Do one thing at a time – don't multi-task. This causes overload and burn-out. Make a decision to always give people your full attention.

14. Learn to be led, rather than to always lead. Choose to trust others – rely on them. You might be surprised.

15. Count your blessings. Be grateful for what you have in your life, rather than always looking for what is missing.

> *"Hateful to me as the gates of Hades is that man who hides one thing in his heart, and speaks another."*
>
> **Homer**

How to Trade God's Value System for My Own

Comparison of Personal Values Thinking

 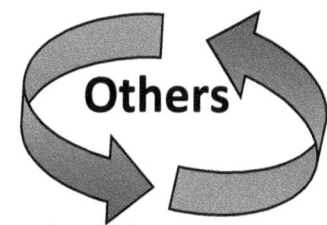 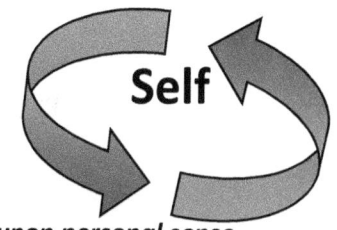

(based upon inner relationship With Holy Spirit/obedience Open/Depth of soul)	(based upon approval of other people/securing oneself through task and performance/conditional)	(based upon personal sense of comfort and satisfaction/ sets terms/ shallow)
Healthy Relationship	**Codependent Relationship**	**Narcissistic Relationship**
"Servant-minded" (kinosis) Philippians 2 example	"Survival-minded" (protective) protective/shielding self	"Selfmade-minded" blinded/lone-ranger
1. Intentional disciple	1. Passive, needy	1. Stoic, has no need
2. **Love-based (Agape)**	2. **Fear-based (reactionary, defensive)**	2. **Pride-based (unfeeling)**
3. Operates within boundaries From relationship/ values others	3. Operates within boundaries in fear of rejection/judgment	3. Values boundaries when agrees with mindset
4. We value others because each person carries the image of God within themselves, whether positively or negatively	4. We value others when they contribute to our own sense of being useful, we become needed/essential.	4. We value others when they agree with our opinion; when they reinforce our own defense patterns.
5. We gauge our value by what God has said about us.	5. We gauge our value by the responses of others.	5. We gauge our value by how comfortable we are.
6. Our treatment of others is based upon the ethics described in God's Word.	6. Our treatment of others is based upon relative opinion, and our personal safety.	6. Our treatment of others is based upon our own desires, goals, & needs.
7. We live by absolutes, with the desire to communicate God's nature and comfort with others.	7. We live by relative absolutes, with the desire to be affirmed and encouraged.	7. We live by relative absolutes, with the desire to do as our appetites dictate.

When God is at the center, what is important to Him becomes important to us – our Heart-values change.

The Twelve Steps of Alcoholics Anonymous –
*could be reworked as **Addicts Anonymous***

The relative success of the A.A. program seems to be due to the fact that an alcoholic who no longer drinks has an exceptional faculty for "reaching" and helping an uncontrolled drinker.

In simplest form, the A.A. program operates when a recovered alcoholic passes along the story of his or her own problem drinking, describes the sobriety he or she has found in A.A., and invites the newcomer to join the informal Fellowship.

The heart of the suggested program of personal recovery is contained in Twelve Steps describing the experience of the earliest members of the Society:

1. We admitted we were powerless over alcohol - that our lives had become unmanageable.
2. Came to believe that a Power greater than ourselves could restore us to sanity.
3. Made a decision to turn our will and our lives over to the care of God as we understood Him.
4. Made a searching and fearless moral inventory of ourselves.
5. Admitted to God, to ourselves and to another human being the exact nature of our wrongs.
6. Were entirely ready to have God remove all these defects of character.
7. Humbly asked Him to remove our shortcomings.
8. Made a list of all persons we had harmed, and became willing to make amends to them all.
9. Made direct amends to such people wherever possible, except when to do so would injure them or others.
10. Continued to take personal inventory and when we were wrong promptly admitted it.
11. Sought through prayer and meditation to improve our conscious contact with God as we understood Him, praying only for knowledge of His will for us and the power to carry that out.
12. Having had a spiritual awakening as the result of these steps, we tried to carry this message to alcoholics and to practice these principles in all our affairs.

Miscellaneous Notes on Codependency

Codependency involves more than one person. It is a relationship that needs change.

Codependents have learned to live with varying degrees of passivity about their lives, and allow their days to be determined for them by outside circumstances and relationships. In order for change to take place, there must be a decision made by the codependent, to take steps toward health, and change.

How to Practically Attack the Problem of Codependency:

1. Establish personal priorities.

2. Set a personal schedule, making time for the priorities you have set for yourself. Make sure to set aside time for personal growth and development, as well as reasonable rest periods.

3. Determine what constitutes each level of relationship in your life.

4. Establish personal boundaries for relationships you find yourself in, assessing the level of communication presently taking place in each of the relationships in your life at the present time.

5. As you walk through these steps, you will find yourself in inner conflict in varying degrees and differing levels. Utilizing the "Lies that Tie us to Oppression" sheet handed out in this workshop, begin to confront the lies you have always thought to keep you "safe," with the Word of God.

Co Dependents have learned to become passive about their own inner life development. Very seldom do they press through to see change come in a situation. They just try to "do better."

Signals of Unhealthy Relational Boundaries

People who struggle with Addiction and Codependency have a difficult time establishing healthy boundaries within their lives. It doesn't help that our society as a whole, has become angry, addicted, demanding and selfish. How is a truly caring person supposed to respond? The first thing we need to do is to realize that our personal wounded-ness has left us with areas within our souls that are too open and too vulnerable. We need to learn how to be graciously assertive, how to actively listen, and how to communicate clearly from an inner life level.

1. Telling everything.

2. Talking on an inner life, or intimate level at a first meeting.

3. Falling in love with a new acquaintance.

4. Falling in love with anyone who expresses care, or reaches out to you; attaching your heart to them.

5. Being overwhelmed by a person – preoccupied with them.

6. Becoming sexual outside of marriage; acting on impulse.

7. Going against personal values, and moral judgments, to gain approval from others.

8. Not noticing another person's boundaries.

9. Not saying "no" when someone invades, or expresses violation of your own boundaries.

10. Reciprocating out of fear of rejection to expressions of care you didn't want.

11. Taking as much as you can get for the sake of getting.

12. Giving as much as you can give for the sake of giving.

13. Allowing someone to take as much as they can from you. Allowing them to use you because you want their approval.

14. Expecting others, and or circumstances to direct your life, without inner awareness or knowledge of the Holy Spirit's guidance to your own heart.

15. Expecting other people to define who you are, rather than your relationship with Jesus Christ.

16. Believing that others should be able to anticipate your needs and desires.

17. Expecting others to be your source – to fill your needs automatically.

18. Falling apart so someone will take care of you.

19. Self Abuse

20. Sexual and physical abuse, Compulsive eating and drug usage.

The Principles of Change

1. There is always hope for change.

2. We cannot change what we do not acknowledge.

3. The primary ingredient of the change process is Truth (in love) in an open heart.

4. We cannot change others. We can only change ourselves.

5. Repentance is the only catalyst (beginning place) for change to occur.

6. Our inner brokenness is the beginning place for repentance, and therefore Change.

7. Changes we seek to make within ourselves without the help of the Holy Spirit, will never be permanent, because they are based in our own works and effort.

8. We cannot expect God to give grace or healing, when we are unwilling to repent.

9. Growth cannot happen without change.

10. Change will involve both forward and backward motion, always with our eyes fixed upon the goal of becoming like Christ.

11. The Doorway into the Change Process is guarded from the inside, by a person who must open the door from the inside. It cannot be forced open.

12. Change must be chosen, sometimes with struggle.

13. Change comes as a result of Training, not as a result of simply trying, using the same tools we have used in the past.

14. Change is a process. It takes time. What took years to tear down will require a season of hard work to redeem, repair and restore.

15. It takes intentional maintenance for change to remain.

©atg/dcg

To Overcome Addiction

1. Repent for Pride – "the refusal to allow God to take care of you."

2. Come to grips with the concept that addiction is sin. It is a search for comfort and relationship outside of the healthy parameters designed by our Creator.

3. Receive the fact that God loves you, even in the place of addiction. Love cannot be earned.

4. Recognize the spiritual and physical dangers associated with habits you have given yourself to. Recognize and admit the deception involved with addiction – that a person can realize fulfillment and connection outside of relationship with God and relationship within a healthy community.

5. Take a hard and truth based look at what the addiction has done to your thinking patterns – how you view others, and how you view yourself.

6. Make a choice – a real choice – to hate the sin, and ask God for the desire to overcome the addiction.

7. Repent wholeheartedly from the sin of addiction, and turn to God for healing, strength and overcoming power. Admit that addiction is a selfish and morally wrong habit and behavior.

8. Choose to step into a healthy community. First, with one trustworthy relationship, and then with a healthy group. Choose to have no secrets. Admit the addiction weakness to those within the group, Choose to live your life in the Light of the Spirit of God, and the body of Christ.

9. Recognize the lies and the "set up" of the enemy within the heart. What did you believe that the addiction would do for you? Why did you continue? Allow God to show you the patterns of thinking that have led to each instance you have fallen into the habit pattern of addiction.

10. Apply the truth of the Word of God to the lies set up within the heart. Seek counsel, and help from a therapist, or a program, to "hold your feet to the fire." Keep yourself accountable for your choices. Learn new patterns for your life, in dealing with rejection, failure, fear and stress.

11. Find new patterns of behavior, through diet, exercise, relaxation, and physical activity. Take action against the thing trying to captivate you. Learn the healthy pattern Father God has designed for your life. Don't allow your old appetites to influence and control your behavior.

12. Utilize the energy once spent indulging the addiction, into fighting against it. Each of these steps will need to be continually repeated and addressed for intentional growth and increasing strength and maturity to occur. Choose to remain a life-long learner; vulnerable and teachable before God.

© dcg/atg

The Twelve Steps of Alcoholics Anonymous –

could be reworked as ***Addicts Anonymous***

The relative success of the A.A. program seems to be due to the fact that an alcoholic who no longer drinks has an exceptional faculty for "reaching" and helping an uncontrolled drinker.

In simplest form, the A.A. program operates when a recovered alcoholic passes along the story of his or her own problem drinking, describes the sobriety he or she has found in A.A., and invites the newcomer to join the informal Fellowship.

The heart of the suggested program of personal recovery is contained in Twelve Steps describing the experience of the earliest members of the Society:

1. We admitted we were powerless over alcohol - that our lives had become unmanageable.
2. Came to believe that a Power greater than ourselves could restore us to sanity.
3. Made a decision to turn our will and our lives over to the care of God as we understood Him.
4. Made a searching and fearless moral inventory of ourselves.
5. Admitted to God, to ourselves and to another human being the exact nature of our wrongs.
6. Were entirely ready to have God remove all these defects of character.
7. Humbly asked Him to remove our shortcomings.
8. Made a list of all persons we had harmed, and became willing to make amends to them all.
9. Made direct amends to such people wherever possible, except when to do so would injure them or others.
10. Continued to take personal inventory and when we were wrong promptly admitted it.
11. Sought through prayer and meditation to improve our conscious contact with God as we understood Him, praying only for knowledge of His will for us and the power to carry that out.
12. Having had a spiritual awakening as the result of these steps, we tried to carry this message to alcoholics and to practice these principles in all our affairs.

Section Six
What Does the Bible Say About Addictions and Codependency?

The Need for Healthy Attachment/Bonding

When I ask a client to consider the form of their family of origin, I usually ask them to draw their own graph of what family life looked like. From there, it is a short step to ask them to describe the "perfect family," or what they wish their childhood had looked like. In cases where Depression extends to the Core, or Inner Child, this proves to be a wonderful exercise in helping them to embrace the need for change; and their own need to experience healthy attachment and bonding.

That being said; many studies have been done over the past twenty years, regarding the effectiveness of healthy bonding during childhood, and its cause/effect in human development. Without fail, the following were shown to be true regarding the process of Healthy Attachment/Bonding in Human Development:

Most prevalently discovered in the studies I have read over the years, Healthy Bonding provides:

- A sense of confidence
- A personal sense of value
- Stronger communication skills
- Healthy gastric and digestion systems
- More ease in relationships as an adult
- A strong conscience (moral determination of absolutes)
- An ability to label and describe emotions and thoughts
- A desire to help others

Among persons who have had impaired bonding experiences, a uniform detachment is manifested. Detached and unfeeling persons, formerly known as "psycho-pathic" in the counseling field, are now referred to as "socio-pathic" or as exhibiting a "social detachment disorder." These labels communicate the difficulty a person who has no sense of healthy attachment experiences when seeking to live in community, or even family life.

The unconditional Love of God, exhibited in the Body of Christ can become a great source of healing for a person in this state. Indeed, when a person commits to become a disciple of Jesus Christ, the Holy Spirit begins the work of developing what I call "relate-ability" within the life. He guides each of us into all Truth, shaping and forming us into the image of Jesus. He helps us to become "rooted and grounded in love." (Ephesians 3:17)

Isn't Co-Dependency A Part of Being a Loving Christian?

It is important that we realize that many Scriptures have been taken out of context, in order to keep the deception of Codependency alive in the Western church.

Galatians 6:1-5
" Brethren, if a man is overtaken in any trespass, you who are spiritual restore such a one in a spirit of gentleness, considering yourself lest you also be tempted. Bear one another's burdens, and so fulfill the law of Christ. For if anyone thinks himself to be something, when he is nothing, he deceives himself. But let each one examine his own work, and then he will have rejoicing in himself alone, and not in another. **For each one shall bear his own load."**

The problem with Codependency is that it causes those who practice it to develop an inflated opinion of their own indispensability. We can seek to help others, but the truth of the matter is that each person has to carry their own responsibility before the Lord. When we approach our lives, seeking to help others before we are obedient to, or seek the Spirit of God, we make ourselves the center, rather than Jesus. God does not expect me to make life "livable" for others.

Romans 14:7-12 (New King James Version)
"For none of us lives to himself, and no one dies to himself. For if we live, we live to the Lord; and if we die, we die to the Lord. Therefore, whether we live or die, we are the Lord's. For to this end Christ died and rose and lived again, that He might be Lord of both the dead and the living. But why do you judge your brother? Or why do you show contempt for your brother? For we shall all stand before the judgment seat of Christ. For it is written:
" As I live, says the LORD, Every knee shall bow to Me, And every tongue shall confess to God." ***So then each of us shall give account of himself to God."***

We each will give account for our own lives. Codependency stops the identity development of the person who practices Codependency. If you have become stuck in your spiritual development, how will you give account of that stagnancy to the Lord?

In light of these materials, then,

How do we respond to Jesus' words in Matthew 25 about how we are to express His love to the world?

How about Ephesians 4:28-32? Let's read them.

Is all care-giving behavior, codependent behavior? Many secular psychologists believe it is, and go so far as to say our entire society is ill. However, there are those who disagree with this mindset, because it is evident that we all have been created with a need for mutual caring and sharing within a community environment.

It is part of Christian character to be concerned with the welfare of others. Philippians 2:3-4

It is part of Christian leadership to become a servant to those around us, in order to show them the love of Jesus.   Matthew 20:25-28

To focus on the problem of Codependency, is to make the goal of my life one of making myself happy. How is that different than the narcissist?

Proverbs 11:2 (King James)
When pride cometh, then cometh shame, but with the lowly (humble) is wisdom."

The base of operation for codependents is **toxic shame (see chart)**. Father God never shames anyone. Another word for shame is condemnation. Sometimes condemnation mixes with a sense of rejection or abandonment, and the person learns to live life with a cynical perspective. (A cynic is a person who looks for something to go wrong in any circumstance.... It has been said that a cynic is a person who looks both ways before crossing a one way street.)

Any time we seek to take control of our own healing, we are taking hold of pride. We are thinking that we are able to heal ourselves. We'll fix it. We'll heal ourselves, and make ourselves acceptable to God.

Humility simply put, is living with an open and vulnerable lifestyle, honestly facing life with an inner life perspective before the Lord.

The Substitution Principle

*Somehow, what we **substitute** for the real thing just isn't as fulfilling as the real thing…..*

Emotional Intimacy= The Real Thing

What have we learned to substitute for healthy relationships? How do we cover our Pain? Note: Each of the substitutes listed below have no ability to fulfill in Life to the same degree as actual community care and bonding/attachment. Substitutions fail, and ignite the processes of discouragement and depression.

Which of the following substitutes have you leaned too heavily upon to survive?

1. **Money /Success –** When a person learns to live in surface areas of IQ only, image becomes extremely important them. The more successful they are, the more achievements they attain, the more money they possess, the more they will become dependent upon those things to determine their value and importance.

   What the Bible says about Money/Success –

   Ecclesiastes 7:12 (NLT)
   "Wisdom and money can get you almost anything, but only wisdom can save your life."

   1 Timothy 6:10 (NKJV) "For the love of money is a root of all kinds of evil. Some people, eager for money, have wandered from the faith and pierced themselves with many griefs."

   Luke 16:13 (NIV) "No one can serve two masters. Either you will hate the one and love the other, or you will be devoted to the one and despise the other. You cannot serve both God and money."

   Matthew 6:19-20 (NIV) "Do not store up for yourselves treasures on earth, where moths and vermin destroy, and where thieves break in and steal. But store up for yourselves treasures in heaven, where moths and vermin do not destroy, and where thieves do not break in and steal.

2. **Conflict Avoidance/Being the "NiceGuy"** – Because a person has been wounded by unhealthy conflict at some point in the past, they might learn to "stuff" their anger, and avoid necessary conflicts. A person might have a misunderstanding of the meaning of boundaries, thinking that establishing a few personal healthy boundaries is wrong behavior, or is selfish. This person then begins to show elements of depression and withdrawal, losing joy in relationships and activities.

   What the Bible says about Conflict Avoidance/Being the "NiceGuy" –

   Matthew 18:15 (NAS) If your brother sins against you, go and show him his fault, just between the two of you. If he listens to you, you have won your brother over.

   Romans 12:18 (NKJV) If it is possible, as much as depends on you, live peaceably with all men.

3. **Expressing Anger/Taking Control –** This person is usually emotionally and relationally un-tooled, and has decided at some point to protect and defend the areas where they are most vulnerable. The problem with choosing this type of substitute is that the person tends to become isolated, and without close relationships.

   What the Bible says about Expressing Anger/Taking Control –

   Romans 16:17 Now I urge you, brethren, note those who cause divisions and offenses, contrary to the doctrine which you learned, and avoid them.

   Psalm 4:4 (NKJV) Be angry, and do not sin. Meditate within your heart on your bed, and be still. Selah

   Proverbs 29:22-23 (NKJV) An angry man stirs up strife, And a furious man abounds in transgression. A man's pride will bring him low, but the humble in spirit will retain honor.

   Matthew 5:22 (NKJV) But I say to you that whoever is angry with his brother without a cause shall be in danger of the judgment. And whoever says to his brother, 'Raca!' *(stupid)* shall be in danger of the council. But whoever says, 'You fool!' shall be in danger of hell fire.

   Ephesians 4:25-27 (NKJV) Therefore, putting away lying, *" Let each one of you speak truth with his neighbor,"* for we are members of one another. *"Be angry, and do not sin"*: do not let the sun go down on your wrath, nor give place to the devil.

   Proverbs 29:11 A fool vents all his feelings, But a wise *man* holds them back.

Ephesians 4:29-32 Let no corrupt word proceed out of your mouth, but what is good for necessary edification, that it may impart grace to the hearers. And do not grieve the Holy Spirit of God, by whom you were sealed for the day of redemption. Let all bitterness, wrath, anger, clamor, and evil speaking be put away from you, with all malice. And be kind to one another, tenderhearted, forgiving one another, even as God in Christ forgave you.

4. **Trying to be perfect *for* God, *without* God –** This person has many times been involved in a structured form of religious piety, usually without experiencing a deep, inner relationships with God. Perhaps their home environment was controlling, or they are justice centered in their life approach, seeing no need for areas of compromise or compatible relationship development.

   What the Bible says about Trying to be perfect for God, without God –

   Mark 12:29-31 Jesus answered him, "The first of all the commandments *is*: 'Hear, O Israel, the LORD our God, the LORD is one. And you shall love the LORD your God with all your heart, with all your soul, with all your mind, and with all your strength.' This *is* the first commandment. And the second, like *it, is* this: 'You shall love your neighbor as yourself.' There is no other commandment greater than these."

   Romans 15:13 Now may the God of hope fill you with all joy and peace in believing, that you may abound in hope by the power of the Holy Spirit.

   Isaiah 61:1-3 The Spirit of the Lord GOD *is* upon Me, Because the LORD has anointed Me to preach good tidings to the poor; He has sent Me to heal the brokenhearted, To proclaim liberty to the captives, And the opening of the prison to *those who are* bound; To proclaim the acceptable year of the LORD, And the day of vengeance of our God; To comfort all who mourn, To console those who mourn in Zion, To give them beauty for ashes, The oil of joy for mourning, The garment of praise for the spirit of heaviness; That they may be called trees of righteousness, The planting of the LORD, that He may be glorified."

   Psalm 147:2-4 The LORD builds up Jerusalem; He gathers together the outcasts of Israel. He heals the brokenhearted And binds up their wounds. He counts the number of the stars; He calls them all by name.

Ephesians 5:16 tells us to redeem the time, because the days are evil. Codependency robs us because:

It ruins our lives, because it causes us to stop being honest.

It is a lot of work to keep everyone happy
(We become peace-keepers, "peace at any cost"
rather than peace-makers – making true and relational peace.)

It allows evil to come in, take more and more ground

It allows good to pass us by. We learn to hide, and be "low impact" people.

It denies our part in the stuff of life – ("People always take advantage of me," instead of "I allow others too much control in my life.")

It stops us from bringing relationships into our inner life.

It stops growth, because it hates conflict. There can be no growth without conflict.

It says that hurt is always evil, but healthy relationships involve hurt – we are called to strengthen each other, and to speak the truth in love.

It creates an atmosphere for guilt, shame and condemnation.

It stops us from taking ownership – and encourages us to criticize.

It opens a door for religiosity – because our passivity is mis-labeled as "piety."

It kills God-given, Father-directed assertiveness

It cultivates rage and anger.

When it is accompanied by inner wounded-ness, it becomes controlling, because it
a) demands that everyone else pick up the load or, it
b) finds identity and approval in being everyone else's savior.

It causes us to become passive. And, passivity means that we have chosen to believe lies in the inner man about how life works.

Ten Steps To Begin the Journey Out Of Co-Dependency

Step One   *Move past denial, and admit that you operate your life in Codependency. Ask the Lord to show you the places in your life where you have become a survivor, and have shut yourself off from healing and wholeness. Establish a daily time of prayer and meditation with Father God.*

Step Two   *Embrace the fact that dysfunctions existed in your family of origin, and that even though those things seemed normal to you as a child, they have led you to the place of co-dependence you find yourself in now. Slow down in your day to day life, and take inventory of the total picture of your childhood, allowing yourself to move from minimization and denial into reality.*

Step Three   *Begin to record your history, not to attempt to re-experience the feelings, but to record the information for the healing process. If intense feelings do come to the surface, beginning to overwhelm you, seek the help of a trustworthy friend or therapist. Choose to trust this person, and allow them into the areas of your heart where the pain has been hidden.*

Step Four   *Move out of passivity. Realize that your adult symptoms of Co-dependency are interfering with your ability to live your life with healthy relationships. Do something about them, or they will continue to undermine your relationships with others, and with yourself. You are the only one who can make the changes that need to be made in your life. Waiting for the "perfect moment" will keep you stuck and perpetuated in co-dependent patterns. This decision is a step to empower you, and restore, or help you to find your inner Voice.*

Step Five   *Realize that taking care of yourself is an act of stewardship; that it is not a selfish act; that you are actually moving out of the bondage of the Fear of Man. Confront the false guilt and shame that have bullied you into picking up elements of control, and choose to have fun, however difficult it might be at first. Remember that Jesus commanded that we love others as we love ourselves.*

Step Six   *Repent for allowing other people's approval and their opinions to govern our security and esteem levels. Open your heart to Father God, and allow His love to come into your heart, without arguing with His forgiveness and mercy for your past mistakes and failures. Receive the love of God inside the walls of protection you have built, and allow His grace to address your fears.*

Step Seven   *Choose to admit that you make mistakes – without denial, without defenses. Choose to let go of your right to be right. Seek to be less vocal about your opinions in dealings with others. Release the control of a situation intentionally, not seeking to correct it or "fix" it if things don't go the way you think they should. Resist the urge to control—Allow other people around you to learn much needed lessons.*

Step Eight   *Choose to embrace the character defects you have utilized to deflect intimacy in your life. (ie., arguing over the facts in discussion, perfectionism, verbal unloading, withdrawal and retreat, blame, having to have the last word, thinking yourself better than others, or superior, etc.). Repent for them, and surrender to the Lord, asking Him to remove them from your life. Make a list of negative qualities that you see in your own life, perhaps from things that were spoken to you by those who wounded you growing up. On a piece of paper, make a left side column with this "self esteem list" of how you see yourself. Then, utilizing the "My Identity in Christ" bookmark included in this workshop packet, confront each of these perceived qualities with the Word of God. Allow the Word of God to speak truth to your heart, and choose to believe the Word rather than your perceptions.*

Step Nine   *Begin to confront within yourself each element of codependence, beginning with boundaries in relationships. Utilize the Twelve Steps from Alcoholics Anonymous, addressing your own addiction to approval and acceptance from those for whom you have become the source person.*

Step Ten   *Choose to make amends and seek forgiveness to those whom you have hurt or wounded in your life up until the present. Seek to establish relationships when possible. Choose to honor and regard the boundaries of others. Open your heart to community and relationship, and as you do, seek to not only set boundaries for yourself and your relationships, but to honor those boundaries as well, keeping your heart and life focused on the purpose and pathway the Holy Spirit has set for you in your daily prayer time. .*

Section Seven
Scriptural Prayer and Supportive Materials

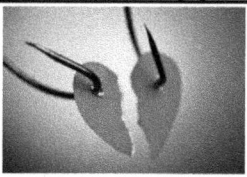

Notes Regarding Bondages

In Biblical terms, a bondage is an action or practice, thought or habit pattern, which a person cannot seem to discipline themselves to bring to an end. Even when they think they have some degree of victory over the problem, a "hunger pang" for a particular experience of sin will act as a handle upon their soul, which Satan uses to pull them back into defeat and condemnation. This in itself is an evidence of demonic influence.

Bondages show themselves in addictions, generational tendencies, and in outright selfish choices. Choices which bind the soul (giving the devil a legal right to hold the person in a cycle of bondage:

1. Promises made, or vows	Deuteronomy 23:21-22 Numbers 30:9
2. Lies which have been told	John 8:32
3. The rejection of abstinence from sexual immorality is actually a rejection of God.	I Thessalonians 4:1-8
4. Anxiety is in the heart because of sin in the heart. (There must a recognition of the need for deliverance.)	Psalm 38:17-22
5. To take counsel other than God's to heart before His counsel is rebellion. a. procrastination is rebellion	Isaiah 30: 1

How Does A Person Break Co-Dependency?

It is important that people who deal with Codependency realize that these tendencies have moved way beyond choosing to serve others, or deciding to live unselfishly. The tendencies to Codependency are based in the desire to please others, in order to gain approval. The person who struggles with Codependency has no core identity that they are able to grasp. They are unable to pinpoint priorities, or place boundaries within their lives, for fear of failing, or for fear of being potentially misunderstood or rejected. Additionally, they have silently chosen to survive by living their lives for or through other people.

Walking a Client Through Forgiveness

When a person battles through Addiction/Codependency, one of the mechanisms feeding the cycling problem is the human tendency to relive experienced past wounding. One of the main steps in the healing journey is the person coming into willingness to forgive.

In the biblical languages, the word "forgive" is the English word, translated from Hebrew and Greek root words which mean "release," or "let go." Forgiveness then, is a person's willingness to release the individual or group of individuals who hurt them. Without forgiveness, an inky black root of Bitterness begins to tap down into the soul. In Hebrews 12:15, the writer urges believers to "looking carefully lest anyone fall short of the grace of God; lest any root of bitterness springing up cause trouble, and by this many become defiled."

Bitterness then, can be caused in a life, when a person does not apply the Grace of God to the wound experienced; only God's Grace can change something bitter into something sweet.

Forgiveness cannot happen flippantly; nor can it take place simply because we want to show ourselves to be dutiful and obedience disciples. It cannot happen devoid of emotion.

Forgiveness is a process. It is a choice which does not happen all at once. The one doing the forgiving must grieve the loss caused by the injury. As the wound is faced, and taken apart, its depth assessed and laid on the sacrificial altar before God, the wounded person then is able to release their injurer with full knowledge of what they are releasing.

This is how closure occurs in the life.

Forgiveness is the means through which we are able to experience reconciliation within the members of our soul. When we pursue the process of becoming able to release another from the debt they owe us, we pursue the core purpose of the discipleship method. We become like Christ Jesus.

Forgiveness is not healing. Many times, we confuse the two, somehow thinking if we just "choose" without emotion, we can shortcut the process. But then we struggle with anger, self-hatred, guilt, and ultimately Depression.

Experiencing the longer pathway allows us to separate the two progressions. Just as a person has to go to the doctor when they experience a stab wound, so a wounded soul must be intentionally assessed, addressed, and brought to a healthy state; many times utilizing therapy and exercises for emotional development.

The journey to forgive the person who wielded the knife, however, is much different. To forgive means giving up the right to keep track of what is owed to us. It means divesting the blame and injustice we feel into the heart and hands of a loving God. He is the Keeper of the Accounts. In Him, everything comes into balance. In fact, the Greek word "logos," which is translated "Word" in John 1:1, is actually a bookkeeping term. It refers to the figures which bring balance to the accounts.

Jesus is the Logos. When we divest our right to hold others accountable, He brings the Balance.

He will always be the Last Word.

On the next few pages, is a set of worksheets I developed to help clients who are walking through the decision to forgive injuries they have experienced. The worksheets are taken from a program for women available through our ministry called, "Ruth and Naomi – The Healing Journey." The workbook is designed to accompany twelve mp3 sessions; both are available through our ministry offices.

God's Balance Sheet of Forgiveness
(adapted from "Ruth and Naomi: The Healing Journey," Chapter 10)

1. Please turn to Matthew 18:21-35. Read the story, and then answer the questions below.

    a. verse 23   Who was responsible to settle the accounts?

    b. verse 24-25 The first slave owed more than $10 million in silver to his master. Even if he and his family were separated and sold, the price they would draw could not come anywhere close to that much. (In earthly terms, the man owed more than his life was worth.)

    c. verse 26   Could the slave pay the debt, in reality?

    d. verse 27   What were the steps of forgiveness, the king walked through? List them here.

           1.

           2.

           3.

2. Read verse 28. The second servant's debt was the equivalent of one day's wage. What blind spot did the first servant have?

    Could he see the relationship between the debt the second servant owed him, and his own debt that had been forgiven?

a. verse 29-30 Was the first servant's heart open to the man who owed him the debt of one day's wage?

b. Was he grateful, really, for his own debt being forgiven?

How can you tell?

c. What would have shown his gratefulness?

d. Read verse 31-25. How does the king view the first servant's injustice in his dealings?

3. What did the king consider to have been a better representation of the king's action and attitude toward indebtedness?

4. What is the end result of the first slave's attitude of unforgiveness?

a. What areas in your own life have experienced torment? List them here.

5. Copy verse 35 here.

6. Take a few moments to journal on a separate piece of paper regarding painful memories and experiences in your past that seem to be "speaking" to you lately.

7. From that journal, please utilize the next few pages and make a list of the injuries, which have been speaking to your soul, and have been "in your face," in regard to pain and trust issues. Please make a bulleted list of those injuries in the left hand column below. Please also name the person who inflicted the injury with the memory, or painful circumstance. If the injury was due to a choice which you made, please list yourself as the person who inflicted injury.

<u>Injuries assignment</u>	<u>Contrast</u>

Injuries assignment | **Contrast**

Injuries	Contrast assignment

8. Our own pain tends to blind us to the needs of others. And our pain is based upon our perception of the situation. Our perceptions are the basis of our reactions and choices.

It is important that we realize that we are not alone – ever. That even when things happen to us that were not the best possible situation – that when we bring that pain and difficulty to Father God, He is able to bring good out of it. He is able to heal. In order to facilitate that process – we must let go of our own perceptions, and allow Him to give us fresh insight and understanding.

Please look up the following scriptures, and please contrasting character qualities that pertain to Father God in the "Contrast Assignment" column, as they relate to the injuries you have listed.

The Scriptures are:

I Corinthians 13

Psalm 103

Psalm 91

Psalm 54:4-5

Psalm 18

Ephesians 2:1-10

9. Meet with a prayer partner and walk through these areas of pain and difficulty, making confession of your heart attitude, and any struggles you may have with releasing the injustices of these situations.

10. Ask your mentor to help you to understand what bondages and difficulties the person who hurt you might have been struggling with, and ask the Lord to give you compassion for them. This is the first step in learning to forgive.

General Prayer for Freedom

Father God, I acknowledge you as my heavenly Father. I understand and believe what the Word of God says about your nature.

Earthly men may hate me, but You love me. Earthly men may seek to violate and control me, but you will never violate my will. Earthly men may have abused me, but I know that there is no end to your mercy and love for me. I know that you desire to make my paths straight, and to bless me. You do not reward me according to my sins, but according to Your own righteousness.

I have a purpose in Your eyes, and You want me to know and understand that purpose. You want to be my strength when I am weak. You want to be my refuge and to deliver me from all evil. You want me to trust in You and be helped.

So, Father God, I choose today, to surrender to Yom will for my life. I choose to be obedient to You. I choose to obey the authority figures you have put into my life. I know they must give account for my soul.

Lord Jesus, I acknowledge and accept Your gift of life for me. Thank you for the provision of your Blood, which is eternal and all powerful, and has no limits in its availability to me. I apply that Blood to my heart and my life. I repent for allowing the influences and powers of darkness to acquire my allegiance. Please forgive me for listening to those voices and giving in to them. Please wash away the false security which has deceived my heart into forsaking You when seeking love and comfort.

Please melt away those chains which I have allowed to overtake my heart. I repent for seeking comfort and escape anywhere but through Your provision of love for me. I turn away from self-reliance and trusting my own flesh, and the flesh of others to guide me. I choose to trust You. I choose to trust Your word to be the complete counsel for my life.

I choose to disregard any suspicious nature which the enemy of my soul, the devil, uses against me to accuse or condemn those You have put in my path to help and bless me and bring me into freedom. I surrender my desire to be in control of my deliverance. I choose to follow with an open and listening heart.

Father, I confess my fear to you. I am afraid of being violated when my walls are taken down. I am afraid the process of destruction will begin all over again. But I know these are threats from the kingdom of darkness, and so I ask for your Perfect love to cast out fear in me in regard to my freedom. Please be the strength of my life and my shield. Please be the strong high tower into which I can run for safety. You are my Helper.

I want to become the person you created me to be.

I acknowledge you as the Restorer of my soul, and I recognize that Satan has stolen from me my purpose, he has lied to me and brought death and destruction to my heart, life and mind.

I hate him with a perfect hatred. I will not allow demonic voices to give me a false sense of security and identity. I choose to hear Your voice, Father God. Please speak to me.

Holy Spirit, I release You within my heart, and I give you full permission to make my life and person a holy and pure vessel for your habitation.

Thank you Lord that you love me. I am your child. I choose Your way.

Prayer to help in Releasing Forgiveness

Father God, thank you for your love for me. I know that you love me unconditionally. I choose to walk in Your ways. Thank you for the gift of your Son, Who died so that I might live forever.

Father, I choose to forgive everyone who has knowingly and unknowingly inflicted hurts and bruises upon my life.

With my will, I will forgive, and I trust You to fill my heart with your love and the feelings of forgiveness in the days to come.

Father, I choose to release my rights to hold on to these hurts and bruises. I choose to confess them to you, and allow you to be the vindicator and Healer of my Heart.

Thank you for your peace. In Jesus' name, Amen.

Christians and Codependency

Is all care-giving behavior, codependent behavior? Many secular psychologists believe it is, and go so far as to say our entire society is ill, and addicted to a need for approval. However, there are those in the counseling/therapy profession who disagree with this mindset, because it is evident that we all have been created with a need for mutual caring and sharing within a community environment.

It is part of Christian character to be concerned with the welfare of others.

> Philippians 2:3-4
>
> *"Let nothing be done through selfish ambition or conceit, but in lowliness of mind let each esteem others better than himself. Let each of you look out not only for his own interests, but also for the interests of others."*

It is part of Christian leadership to become a servant to those around us, in order to show them the love of Jesus.

> Matthew 20:25-28
>
> *But Jesus called them to Himself and said, "You know that the rulers of the Gentiles lord it over them, and those who are great exercise authority over them. Yet it shall not be so among you; but whoever desires to become great among you, let him be your servant. And whoever desires to be first among you, let him be your slave— just as the Son of Man did not come to be served, but to serve, and to give His life a ransom for many."*

To not be concerned about the welfare of others, is to seek to live as an island. On even a secular level, we should be concerned about the effects of our behavior on those we come in contact with – taking care of customers, giving people what they pay for, being honest in my dealings.

On a personal discipleship level, my life motivation must be set in according to my beliefs and priorities, with Jesus' concerns for my life at the forefront of my attention. When I give my life to Jesus, it is no longer my own. Therefore, the life I am called to live, then, is His life through me; doing what He would do, and saying what He would say. (Galatians 2:20)

By a secular definition, Teresa of Calcutta was a codependent and very diseased, because she accommodated the needs of others with the focus and energies of her life......to the point that her entire identity was swallowed up in the needs of the dying. And herein lies the question: Is that Codependency, or is it ministry?

So, when does Codependency become dangerous for the Christian?

By definition, co-dependency indicates a dependency, or addiction of its own. It is a by-product of an under-developed, or non-developed identity, with care-taking practices providing and sense of worth and value to soothe broken areas of the soul.

In a sense, the co-dependent has learned to take on a serving role in the relationship, looking for approval and a sense of being loved. A person will, after a time, become so entrenched in these behaviors, that they resist change; they are convinced that this form of slavery is their established purpose for living.

The difficulty arises when a codependent person
- (a) realizes they are unable to continue to carry yet one more responsibility, and/or
- (b) their own fragility meets with circumstances that revisit their own pain, and they come to a place of emotional and mental anguish, if not breakdown.

In secular circles, – intervention, confrontation, and detachment, have been heralded as the methods for dealing with the codependent behaviors. These practices are good for those who are married to, or attached to people with addictions (or narcissism), because they represent the only methods of communicating clearly so as to be understood and acknowledged by the addict/narcissist.

"When an alcoholic/ narcissist is married to a loving and caring spouse, the spouse's love and care can be sucked in like a black hole. It can drain the caring spouse of everything they have, leaving them not only exhausted, but also having failed to meet their sick spouse's needs. In these cases, the non-addict spouse must emotionally detach themselves, or they will be become emotionally (and sometimes physically) destroyed." Those non-addicts who find themselves in this situation, usually allow it to continue, because there are convinced that their own lives will be seen to be a failure should they draw a boundary and stop allowing themselves to be used in this way. It is the fear of this failure that ties many codependents into the bondage of their spouse's addiction/narcissism.

However, outside of the codependent/addict relationship, or codependent/narcissist relationship, these practices of defensive confrontation, can become expressions of a twisted form of selfishness and communicate narcissism of their own. Many codependents are *not* in relationships with addicts, *or* narcissists. Their codependent behaviors have become a form of personal selfishness and control, and have taken on a life of their own. In these situations, the control of the helm for the direction of the family, marriage, business is what is at stake, rather than the health and well-being of an individual struggling with an addiction. What is now being called the "Codependency Movement," in most publications, veils a controlling feminism, squarely placing the blame for all of society's ills at the feet of "mean and abusive" men.

It is dangerous to call care-giving behavior a disease. If we were to look just past that label, we would see children abandoned by overwhelmed mothers, churches berated by overloaded ministers, parents accused by rebellious teenagers, and many other ungodly abuses, practiced in the name of "being honest about feelings." The call to give care and to serve was given by Jesus Himself, and it serves as a plumb-line for the definition of Christian character.

The difficulty with Codependency comes when we make ourselves, or others, the Source. When we seek healing without the Healer, or worse, we come with our own answers, we then take on a savior complex. In becoming our own saviors, determining what we need to find our own healing, outside of the Spirit of God, then we become narcissists ourselves. We become blinded to the needs of others, and able to only view our own pain.

Then, we begin to cycle between the two mindsets, unable to come to sure footing. To quote John Calvin, "I cannot know myself, until I know God." The answer to co-dependency is surrender. Surrender to the Spirit of God, and repentance for seeking to prove that we could do things on our own.

If when I serve others, I expect them to acknowledge my sacrifice, or cheer and give accolades, I have not served Christ. I have served myself. This is selfishness.

If when I give care, I expect those around me to cheer me, and tell me what great insight I have received, and recognize my spirituality, I have not served Christ. I have served myself. This is pride.

If when I disagree with someone or I experience correction, I retreat into a bubble, believing myself to be a victim of mistreatment, I have not served Christ. I have served myself. This is a lack of teachability.

If when my desires and needs are not met, I expect someone to notice my sadness and somehow make a miracle happen, and give me a happy ending, I have not sought Christ. I have sought man. This is evidence that I love myself more than I love Christ.

The Christian disciple's focus of heart must be upon Jesus. The Christian disciple's trust for well-being must be centered upon Christ. When we look to others to meet our needs, or to give us approval, or to satisfy our expectations, we have ceased looking to Jesus for answers.

Codependency is the earmark of self-saviorhood. Here are its symptoms:
- Inability to know what "normal" is
- Difficulty in following a project through
- Difficulty having fun
- Judging self, and others without mercy
- Low self-esteem, often projected onto others (They need to get their act together)
- Difficulty in developing or sustaining meaningful relationships
- Believe that others have caused or are responsible for the codependent's emotions

- Over-reacting to change (or intense fear of/ inability to deal with change)
- Inability to see alternatives to situations, thus responding impulsively
- Constantly seeking approval and affirmation, yet having compromised sense of personhood
- Feelings of being different from everyone else.
- Confusion and sense of inadequacy
- Being either super responsible or super irresponsible (can alternate)
- Lack of self confidence in making decisions. No empowerment to choose
- Feeling of fear, insecurity, inadequacy guilt, hurt and shame (all of these are felt and denied to others)
- Isolation and fear of people, resentment of authority figures
- Hypersensitivity to criticism
- Being addicted to excitement/ drama (creating chaos)
- Dependency upon others and a fear of abandonment
- Avoidance of relationships to guard against abandonment fears
- Confusion between love and pity
- Tendency to look for "victims" to help
- Rigidity and need to control (bring order)
- Lies, when it would be just as easy to tell the truth

Co-dependents often use language like "you make me feel _____', or "I was made to feel like _____." (No one can make you feel anything. We choose to feel what we feel.)

All of these symptoms are signals for a need for surrender to the Spirit of God.

Co-Dependency Worksheet – Recovery

1. Please list the methods the person in the center of your personal orbit uses to express his displeasure with you. How do they communicate with you that something isn't going the way they want it to?

2. Please list the methods you use to facilitate that person's behaviors. In other words, what do you do in reaction to the disapproval you feel is coming from that person?

3. Looking at the list of compensating behaviors you have listed above, please consider each performance in your relationship to this person carefully. Which of these behaviors would you say were present in your life before you met this person?

4. Still considering the behaviors listed in question number 2, please consider which behaviors have developed after your relationship with this person began...
Take time to consider ----- What triggered those behaviors?

5. In thinking about the behaviors you have adopted in order to cope with the person in the center of your orbit, what do you wish you had the power to change?

6. Are you angry with this person?

7. Please make a list here of the areas you find yourself repeatedly becoming angry with this person over – even if those areas of situations and feelings you have not communicated with them. It will help you to be able to put them on paper...

8. What personal needs of your own have you sensed "waiting" during the tenure of your relationship with this person?

9. Do you feel trapped?

10. What are you afraid will happen if you address change with this person in any area?

Human Core Desires for Healthy Relationships

1. To be noticed — I Samuel 16:7
2. To be complimented — Ephesians 4:32

3. To be seen — Genesis 16:6-13
4. To be included — Ephesians 2:1-10
5. To be safe (physically) — Psalm 62:8
6. To be affirmed — Psalm 116:1-9

~~~~~~

7. To experience safe touch — Luke 4:18/ Ps. 147:3
8. To be heard (to connect) — Isaiah 1:18
9. To belong (in a group) — Psalm 116:1-9
10. To be received — Psalm 34:15

11. To be trusted (emotionally safe) — James 2:23/Ex 33:11
12. To be chosen — Jeremiah 31:3
13. To be understood (to reciprocate connect) — Psalm 139
14. To be wanted — Ephesians 1:6

~~~~~~

15. To be secure — Psalm 103:8-12/Ps. 18:6-19
16. To be preferred — John 15:15
17. To be wanted — Ephesians 1:3-5

©dg/atg

Suggested Reading List – Addictions and Codependency

1. **Codependent No More: How to Stop Controlling Others and Start Caring for Yourself by** Melody Beattie. (ISBN: 978-089486405) Published by Hazelden House, 1986. 276 pages

2. **Beyond Codependency: And Getting Better All the Time** by Melody Beattie (ISBN: 978-0894865831) Published by Hazelden House, 1989. 252 pages

3. **The New Codependency: Help and Guidance for Today's Generation** by Melodie Beattie (ISBN: 978-1429102145) Published by Simon and Schuster, 2009) 288 pages

4. **Boundaries: When to Say Yes, How to Say No to Take Control of Your Life Paperback** by Henry Cloud and John Townsend (ISBN: 978-0310247456) Published by Zondervan Publishing, 1992) 320 pages

5. **Addictions: A Banquet in the Grave: Finding Hope in the Power of the Gospel (Resources for Changing Lives)** by Edward T. Welch (ISBN: 978-0875526065) Published by P & R Publishing, 2001) 298 pages

6. **Breaking Addiction: A 7-Step Handbook for Ending Any Addiction** by Lance M., M.D. Dodes (Usbn: 978-0061987397) Published by Harper Perennial, 2011. 240 pages

7. **12 Stupid Things That Mess Up Recovery: Avoiding Relapse through Self-Awareness and Right Action** by Allen Berger, Ph.D (ISBN: 978-1592854868) Published by Hazelden House, 2008. 136 pages

8. **A Biblical Guide to Counseling the Sexual Addict Paperback** by Steve Gallagher (ISBN:978-0971547094) Published by Pure Life Ministries, 2005. 208 pages.

9. **Quick-Reference Guide to Addictions and Recovery Counseling, The: 40 Topics, Spiritual Insights, and Easy-to-Use...** by Dr. Tim Clinton and Dr. Eric Scalise (ISBN: 978-0801072321) Published by Baker Books, 2013. 368 pages

10. **Why Does He Do That? Inside the Minds of Angry and Controlling Men** by Lundy Bancroft. (ISBN 978-0425191651) Published by Berkley Books, Reprint edition, 2003. 432 pages

More from Awakened to Grow...

Be sure to complete your set of ATG's handbooks from **A Christian Counselor's Primer On...** series. Titles include Depression, Communication, Fear and Anxiety, Processing Grief, and many more!

Each reference tool contains charts and assessments for personal discovery and development. Recorded teaching sessions are available for each handbook. Just contact us through our website! Handbooks vary in length and are priced at $20 each. *(Published, 2014)*

Elements of Identity Formation – Outlines and charts help the student understand the process of emotional and spiritual identity formation. Especially helpful for all those who struggle with understanding how to experience the love of God on a personal level. Recorded teaching sessions are available for each handbook. Just contact us through our website!

Workbook is available on amazon.com and lulu.com

journey – a novel; The real story of a girl called "Magdalene." A compelling weaving of historical and Biblical events, this painstakingly researched account of the life of Mary Magdalene will surprise you in how it relates to our present culture and your own personal history. 504 pages *(2nd edition)* $33.50 (MSRP) (Published, 2009 & 2014) *Available at amazon.com and/or lulu.com*

Secrets for Relational Living -- For every person who wants to experience healthy relationships! This 8 session class can be studied individually or with a group. Video sessions of the teachings are available through our website. Especially helpful for all those who feel inwardly insecure in successfully communicating and relating to others.

Available on amazon.com and lulu.com

The Chronicles of Hausse – Book One; The Trouble with Dragons -- An allegorical adventure, set in the mystical land of Hausse; where Lightbearers and Demons can be seen and danger lurks around every corner! Written to explain the spiritual realm to middle school and high school aged students, this book has received rave reviews from readers from 8 to 80!

368 pages $22.00 (MSRP) (Published, 2012) *Available at amazon.com and/or lulu.com*

For a more complete listing, please check out our listings on Amazon.com and lulu.com. Please also see our worship/music resources on iTunes.

www.ingramcontent.com/pod-product-compliance
Lightning Source LLC
Chambersburg PA
CBHW080340170426
43194CB00014B/2637